The Guide for Credit Unions Providing Investment and Insurance Services

Guy A. Messick

Copyright © 2019 Guy A. Messick

All rights reserved.

ISBN:

CONTENTS

	Acknowledgments	i
1	Glossary of Terms	1
2	Investment Services	11
3	Insurance Services	39
4	Appendix	51

ACKNOWLEDGEMENTS

I thank colleagues in the credit union, securities, and insurance industries who help me understand how the three disciplines work independently and together to provide valuable services to members. I thank my law partners and family who have tolerated my travel schedule to represent my clients. I am grateful to the late John Unangst, former president of Franklin Mint Federal Credit Union and Chair of the NACUSO Board, who connected me to the credit union and CUSO world.

The Guide for Credit Unions Providing Investment and Insurance Services

CHAPER 1
GLOSSARY OF TERMS

Advisory Firm – This is a firm that is registered to offer Investment Advisory Services. The Advisory Firm can be licensed nationally by the SEC through the Investment Advisors Act of 1940 if the Advisory Firm has at least $100 million of customer assets under management. Advisory Firms with less than $100 million must obtain a state Advisory Firm registration. Advisory Firms are also referred to as Registered Investment Advisory Firms or RIA's.

Advisory Services – Per a written advisory agreement, an advisor provides financial planning services and/or ongoing investment advice and recommendations to customers. The financial advisor makes investment recommendations within the parameters and the risk tolerance established by the customer. The Advisory Services may be *discretionary* meaning that the customer grants the advisor the authority to make all investment decisions. Alternatively, the Advisory Services are *non-discretionary* meaning that each trade must be approved by the customer. Advisory fees vary and may include a flat fee in the case of financial planning or a percent of assets under management for ongoing advice. The customer must also pay for trade execution unless the account is a "wrap account" whereby execution fees and advisory fees are wrapped into one management fee. There may be fees imposed by the product provider for the investment held by the customer, such as mutual fund expenses.

Broker/Dealer - This is a firm that acts as broker to buy and sell securities (stocks, bonds, mutual funds, etc.) on behalf of customers and acts as dealer if the firm buys securities in a proprietary account before selling to customers. Broker/Dealers are required to be (i) a member of the Financial Industry Regulatory Authority (FINRA), a non-government regulator authorized by Congress, (ii) registered with the U. S. Securities and Exchange Commission, a federal regulator, and (iii) a Securities Investor Protection Corporation (SIPC) member. The Broker/Dealer's services are provided through its Registered Representatives who are licensed and regulated by FINRA. Note that Registered Representatives provide brokerage services through a Broker/Dealer. Financial Advisors provide Advisory Services through an Advisory Firm.

<u>*Chubb Letter*</u> – This is the SEC's No-Action Letter to the Chubb Securities Corporation dated November 24, 1993 which states that the SEC will permit Broker/Dealers to pay a financial institution a share of brokerage and advisory commissions even though the financial institution is not registered as a Broker/Dealer or Advisory Firm. Reliance on the <u>Chubb Letter</u> requires that specific conditions and procedures must be met by both the Broker/Dealer and the financial institution as described more fully in this No-Action Letter.

Clearing Firm – This is a Broker/Dealer with the ability to execute trades on the major stock exchanges. Some Broker/Dealers serving credit unions use a third-party Clearing Firm and some self-clear the trades.

Discretionary Services – The customer provides written approval for the Investment Representative to make investment decisions on the customer's behalf within the client's investment goals and risk tolerance without the requirement to obtain customer approval for each transaction.

Dual Employee Plan – This is a Networking Arrangement wherein the Investment Representatives are W-2 employees of the credit union and licensed independent contractors of the Broker/Dealer (the Dual Employee term is a bit of a misnomer). The credit union is paid more of the GDC than in the Managed Plan Programs as the credit union has the responsibility to pay the Investment Representative and the associated costs (e.g., professional liability insurance premiums and continuing education requirements).

Financial Advisor – This is a person who provides financial planning and/or ongoing investment Advisory Services to customers for a fee. Financial Advisors may also be called Investment Advisors and must be affiliated with an Advisory Firm. In additional to being registered with the SEC, Investment Advisory Representatives are often licensed with FINRA as Registered Representatives (see definition below) to provide brokerage services through a Broker/Dealer.

Financial Institution Regulatory Authority ("FINRA") – FINRA is a private non-profit organization established by the securities industry and authorized by Congress to create and enforce rules and regulations for Broker/Dealers and their Registered Representatives to protect investors and maintain the integrity of the securities markets.

Fixed Annuity – A fixed annuity is a type of annuity contract that allows for the accumulation of capital on a tax-deferred basis. In exchange for a lump sum of capital, a life insurance company credits the annuity account with a guaranteed fixed rate of interest while guaranteeing the principal investment. A Fixed Annuity is an insurance product.

Gross Dealer Concession ("GDC") – This is the amount of commission and fees generated from all investment, insurance and advisory products and transactions. The GDC is shared among the Broker/Dealer, Investment Representative and the credit union. The proportion shared varies and is governed by the terms of the Networking Agreement and the Investment Representative's commission schedule both of which are negotiated between the parties.

Insurance Agency – This is an entity that is licensed by a state to sell insurance products and is appointed as an agency to sell by the respective Insurance Carriers.

Insurance Agent – This is the person who sells insurance products in association with an Insurance Agency.

Insurance Broker – This is a person with the required individual license who associates with the Insurance Agency and enables the Insurance Agency to have an entity license.

Insurance Carrier – This is an insurance company that issues insurance policies and takes on the risk of the insurance coverage and benefits payments.

Investment Representative – This person is, for purposes of this Guide, a Registered Representative and/or a Financial Advisor.

Licensed Assistant – This is a person who has a securities license to assist a high performing Investment Representative.

Typically, the Licensed Assistant may only have a FINRA Series 6 license. However, some Licensed Assistants may also have a FINRA Series 7 license. Unlike an unlicensed assistant, a Licensed Assistant can provide advice within the scope of their license. Licensed Assistants may serve customers with lower investment balances.

Managed Plan – This is a Networking Arrangement between the Broker/Dealer and credit union whereby the Broker/Dealer manages the investment Program on behalf of the credit union. It is a turn-key type of model. In a typical Managed Plan the Investment Representatives are either employees or independent contractors of the Broker/Dealer and assigned to work with a specific credit union. The credit union is paid less of the GDC than in the Dual Employee Plan Programs as the Broker/Dealer has the responsibility to pay the Investment Representative and the associated costs (e.g., professional liability insurance premiums and continuing education requirements). The credit union provides marketing support for the Program.

National Credit Union Administration ("NCUA") – This is the federal agency that supervises federally chartered credit unions and administers the federal deposit insurance known as the National Credit Union Share Insurance Fund. NCUA also has some regulatory authority over state-chartered credit unions that have federal deposit insurance.

NCUA General Counsel Opinions ("GCO") – These are published opinions by NCUA General Counsel interpreting the NCUA Rules and Regulations.

Networking Agreement – This agreement defines the relationship between a Broker/Dealer and credit union whereby the Broker/Dealer provides non-deposit investment products (a "*Networking Arrangement*"). The Broker/Dealer pays the credit union a portion of the GDC for providing marketing and administrative assistance to the affiliated Broker/Dealer per the terms set forth in the <u>Chubb Letter</u>. The Networking Agreement is the term used by the SEC but the agreement itself is often called a "Financial Services Agreement."

Non-Discretionary Services - This describes the relationship where the transactions recommended by an Investment Representative to a customer may not be executed unless and until they are approved by the customer.

Office of Supervisory Jurisdiction ("OSJ") – This is the office or person that is the Broker/Dealer's compliance person for the Program at the credit union The OSJ is often referred to as the Registered Principal. The Registered Principal is responsible for assuring that Investment Representatives under their supervision are in compliance with all federal, state, and FINRA rules and regulations as well as the Broker/Dealer's policy and procedures. In credit union investment Programs, the OSJ service can be provided by the Broker/Dealer at the Broker/Dealer's main office, or through a Dual Employee assigned to the branch office located at a credit union.

Platform Representative – This is a person who works full time for the credit union providing credit union services, often a branch or assistant branch manager. The Platform Representative typically only has a FINRA Series 6 license and possibly an insurance license as well.

Program – This is a reference for a credit union's investment Program in affiliation with a Broker/Dealer and/or an Advisory Firm through a Networking Agreement.

Program Manager – This is the person in the Program appointed by the credit union who manages the Investment Representatives' time to meet the needs of members and optimize the sales opportunities. The Program Manager interacts with the Broker/Dealer, the credit union's management and the credit union's marketing department to develop and implement the marketing plan for investment services. The Program Manager is not required to hold a securities license; however, there is value if the Program Manager is licensed and has experience in the securities industry. In some Programs, the Registered Principal is the Program Manager.

Protocol Agreement – This is an industry trade agreement created in 2004 by Broker/Dealers which permits Investment Representatives to take customer contact information with them when they switch firms and solicit customers, provided the agreed procedures are followed. The <u>Protocol Agreement</u> is only effective if both the Investment Representative's new Broker/Dealer and former Broker/Dealer are signatories.

Registered Principal – This is the licensed Intvestment Representative assigned to the investment Program by the Broker/Dealer to provide the OSJ services.

Registered Representative – This is a person licensed by FINRA to sell securities products in association with a Broker/Dealer. The most common FINRA licenses are as follows:

- Series 6 permits licensees to sell mutual funds, variable annuities (if they also hold a life insurance license) and unit investment trusts.

    - Series 7 is a general securities license. Licensees can sell common and preferred stock, options, bonds, mutual funds, variable annuities (if they also hold a life insurance license) and unit investment trusts.

- Series 63 is the Uniform Securities Agent License for state securities licenses. The Series 6 and 7 licensees must have Series 63 as well.
- Series 65 is required for Financial Advisors.
- Series 66 is the combination of Series 63 and 65.
- Series 24 is a license for a Registered Principal. This is needed for the person overseeing the operations of an office who serves as the supervising officer for the Program (OSJ). The Registered Principal must also have all licenses held by the people he or she is supervising.

Securities and Exchange Commission ("SEC") – This is the federal government agency that regulates the sale of securities in the United States. States also have securities commissions that regulate securities sales within their states. If there is conduct by the Broker/Dealers or their Investment Representatives that violates a regulation or poses a threat to the integrity of the securities business, the SEC and/or FINRA may take action which could mean heavy fines, license suspension or expulsion from the industry.

Self-Directed Services – This is a service that permits a customer to buy securities products without obtaining advice from an Investment Representative (e.g., E*Trade).

Variable Annuity – A Variable Annuity is a type of annuity contract that allows for the accumulation of capital on a tax-deferred basis. As opposed to a fixed annuity that offers a guaranteed interest rate and a minimum payment, Variable Annuities offer investors the opportunity to generate higher rates of returns by investing in equity and bond subaccounts. If a

Variable Annuity is annuitized for income, the income payments can vary based on the performance of the subaccounts. A Variable Annuity is a combination of an insurance product and a securities product.

CHAPTER 2
INVESTMENT SERVICES

Why Provide Investment Services?

Credit union members are likely already investing in non-deposit investments products such as stock, bonds, and mutual funds. These investments often constitute a larger portion of a member's financial assets versus bank account balances. The 2013 Federal Reserve Board Study of Consumer Finances showed that for every dollar that a person has on deposit with a financial institution, the person has $4 to $5 invested in retirement accounts, stocks or mutual funds. Members do not deposit all their money in the credit union. They have both deposit dollars and investment dollars. The old objection that investment services will drain a member's share account has been disproven.

Credit unions that provide non-deposit investment products and services are better fulfilling the mission of credit unions to assist members with their financial needs and goals. Additionally, the profits generated by the credit union from an investment Program benefit the members by providing income to the credit union to help pay for other member services. Credit unions can make substantial fee income from financial services. I know a credit union that was able to offset its loan losses in the financial crisis from the fee income earned from investment services. The net income from investment fees should not be understated. The amount of capital and risk needed in a Networking Arrangement with a Broker/Dealer to generate $1 million in fee income from GDC is minimal compared to the capital needed and the associated credit risk to generate $1 million in loan interest.

Studies have found that members who use the credit union's investment services tend to use more credit union products and have more wallet share with the credit union. For example, a survey by the consulting firm of Kehrer Bielan in 2015 compared the difference in primary bank and credit union services utilization for customers/members who have purchased an investment product from the financial institution's investment services Program compared to customers/members who have not purchased an investment product. A sampling of the results are as follows (the investment services customers/members always being the higher number): credit cards 53.8% vs. 34.1%, first mortgage loan 25.7% vs. 11.6%, vehicle loans or leases 21.8% vs. 6.1%, average deposit account balance $8,374 vs. $6,090 and average savings account balance $28,000 vs. $11,700.

If a member wants to withdraw funds from the credit union to buy equities, there are plenty of Broker/Dealers from which to choose. Why not offer the members a convenient alternative and capture a large portion of the commissions generated by these investments? Credit unions not providing investment services are missing out on service and income opportunities. Non-interest income from investment services is dependable income that will never be stopped by a regulator as being predatory or unfair (e.g., overdraft fees and interchange fees).

How Investment Services are Offered?

Networking Arrangements

The typical model is a Networking Arrangement. A credit union enters into a Networking Agreement with a Broker/Dealer to allow the Broker/Dealer and the credit union to jointly market non-deposit investment services to credit union members. Per federal and most state financial privacy laws, a joint marketing arrangement between financial institutions (a Broker/Dealer is considered a financial institution) enables the credit union to share member information without requiring an opt-out term, provided the credit union's privacy policy and privacy notice to its members confirms this information sharing arrangement. A credit union also provides marketing, endorsements, teller referrals and office space in branches. For that support, the Broker/Dealer pays the credit union a portion of the gross dealer concession earned by the Broker/Dealer. This is permitted under the SEC's Chubb Letter.

Advisory Services

Credit unions can also offer Advisory Services (a) as part of the Networking Arrangement with a Broker/Dealer, (b) through fee sharing arrangements with a separate third party Advisory Firm or (c) through a CUSO that is licensed as an Advisory Firm. Most investment firms have plans to move a larger portion of their business to the advisory model which has a steady fee income flow as opposed to the volatility of the transaction-based model. The advisory model is more consistent with the consultative relationship credit unions have with their members. Since the fees go up and down depending on the performance and size of the portfolio, the interests between the

Financial Advisors and their customers in the advisory model are more aligned than in the transaction-based model where Registered Representatives are sometimes accused of churning (i.e., engaging in transactions just to generate fees).

Some credit unions form CUSOs to be licensed as Advisory Firms, which is permitted in NCUA's CUSO Regulations (Part 712.5(l)). A few credit unions only provide Advisory Services. A few credit unions provide Advisory Services in a CUSO but also have a Networking Agreement with a Broker/Dealer. Most credit unions permit the Broker/Dealer to use its affiliated Advisory Services firm if members want Advisory Services.

Broker/Dealer CUSOs

A small number of credit unions have formed CUSOs to be licensed as Broker/Dealers which are also permitted in the NCUA's CUSO Regulations. As you can imagine the costs and the regulatory burdens are significant. Most credit unions do not have the scale to justify the cost of creating a Broker/Dealer, especially when a credit union can earn up to 92% of the GDC in a Networking Arrangement. Navy Federal Credit Union is one of the few credit unions that owns a Broker/Dealer CUSO to serve its members. The Navy FCU Broker/Dealer CUSO outsources many of the operational functions to CUSO Financial Services. Even with Navy's scale, Navy is using a collaboration model to reduce the cost of operating a Broker/Dealer.

A reason why some credit unions consider forming a CUSO to be a Broker/Dealer is to acquire non-member business, often by purchasing the accounts of a highly successful independent Investment Representative who is near retirement age. The customer base of a CUSO can be 49% non-members. Once the customers of the highly successful Investment

Representatives are associated with the Broker/Dealer CUSO, the CUSO will receive the commission share and the credit union can cross sell its services. The 51% credit union member customer base requirement can be managed by (a) having other Investment Representatives in the Program with a high credit union member customer base and (b) by a concentrated effort to convert as many non-member customers to credit union membership.

You may hear the term "shell" Broker/Dealer as a lower cost option to form a Broker/Dealer CUSO. The name is misleading as the CUSO is for all purposes a Broker/Dealer. It just means that the CUSO outsources as many of the functions it can to an independent Broker/Dealer as a service provider. The Investment Representatives are registered with the independent Broker/Dealer and all sales are through the independent Broker/Dealer. The CUSO, as the referring Broker/Dealer, receives a portion of the commissions. However, there are certain key positions that you cannot outsource such as Registered Principal. Thus a "shell" Broker/Dealer is still expensive but not as expensive as absorbing all the costs internally. Unless there is a plan to acquire a significant amount of non-member business, the Networking Arrangement is more cost effective.

The Rules

Credit unions do not have the power to sell securities products, so they must partner with a Broker/Dealer or create a Broker/Dealer CUSO. The SEC and FINRA regulate the sale of securities nationally. The states also have their own security regulators, but most states do not interfere with the SEC's rules for Networking Arrangements. If there is conduct by the

Broker/Dealers or their Investment Representatives that violates a regulation or poses a threat to the integrity of the securities business, the SEC and/or FINRA will take action which could mean heavy fines or the suspension or expulsion from the industry.

Because control over the participants in the industry is so important, the SEC does not permit any unlicensed companies or persons to receive commissions except for the carve-out for financial institutions in Networking Arrangements. The SEC issued a No-Action Letter to the Chubb Securities Corporation on November 24, 1993 which states that the SEC will permit Broker/Dealers to pay financial institutions a share of commissions even though the financial institution is not registered. The author of the Chubb Letter, Catherine McGuire, then Chief Counsel of the SEC, told me that the reason why the SEC permitted this practice is the SEC's confidence that if there were any issues in the Networking Arrangement, the SEC could enlist the aid of the financial institution's regulator to resolve the issue.

There are conditions that must be met in the Chubb Letter in order to share commissions with the financial institution. The first is that the Broker/Dealer must have exclusive control over the sale of securities and the Investment Representatives, including the compensation arrangement with the Investment Representatives. There must be disclosures provided to, and acknowledged by, the customers stating that the customers understand that the securities sales are being offered by the Broker/Dealer and not the financial institution and the investments are not guaranteed by deposit insurance. If any referral fees are paid to non-licensed employees of the financial institution, the fees must be of nominal value and can only be a one-time fee not contingent upon a sale being made. The industry has used $25 as the maximum referral fee. Non-licensed employees of the financial institution may not provide any investment advice which includes a personal endorsement of a specific security or mutual fund. The terms of the services must be set forth in a written Networking Agreement between the Broker/Dealer and the financial institution. The Broker/Dealer must monitor the activities to ensure compliance with the conditions.

The above rules imposed by the SEC are mirrored and expanded in guidance issued by NCUA and FINRA. NCUA issued a Letter to Federal Credit Union on the subject; Letter Number 150 in December 1993. Letter 150 was replaced in December 2010 with Letter Number 10-FCU-03. FINRA Rules 3160 provides guidance to Broker/Dealers consistent with the Chubb Letter. In summary, the rules require (a) a separation of the areas in branches where investments are sold from the area where deposits are taken, (b) disclosures that clarify the investments are being sold by Broker/Dealer, (c) disclosures that state the investments are not products of the financial institution and not covered by deposit insurance, (d) disclosures that state there is a risk of loss of principal in the investment products, and (e) the prohibition of the credit union's non-licensed employees giving investment advice. There is also a requirement that the disclosures be acknowledged in writing by the customer upon the account opening. While a Letter to Credit Unions is technically guidance only and not a regulation, NCUA expects credit unions to comply with the terms.

The Gramm-Leach-Bliley Act of 1999 required the SEC to codify the networking rules for banks which the SEC finally did in October 2007. The regulation is called Regulation R. Regulation R does not apply to credit unions. Ms. McGuire advised us that the Chubb Letter terms continue to be the sole authority for credit unions to receive a share of commissions in Networking Arrangements.

Prior to 2001, credit unions formed CUSOs to enter into Networking Arrangements with Broker/Dealers. This was because the NCUA Rules and Regulations only permitted a credit union to be paid its actual out-of-pocket expenses in such arrangements. CUSOs were permitted to provide securities brokerage services and thus could enter into Networking Agreements and be paid a share of commissions without such limitation. The <u>Chubb Letter</u> provided that "required service corporations" could be a signatory and payee in the Networking Arrangements. Both credit unions and savings and loan associations under their respective regulations needed separate organizations to accept the commission payments. In 2001, the NCUA passed the <u>Incidental Powers Regulation</u> that permitted credit unions to receive fees from third party service providers without the reimbursement of cost restriction (per the Finder Activities Power).

Serving as a member of the CUNA Task Force for Investment Services in 2001, I attended a meeting with Ms. McGuire at the SEC on the subject. She made it very clear that the Networking Agreements must be with the credit unions and not the CUSOs. CUSOs were no longer "required" to overcome a regulatory hurdle. CUSOs are not regulated by the NCUA. As a result, the SEC wanted the credit union and not the CUSO to be a party to the Networking Arrangement to enable the SEC to seek the assistance of the NCUA to enforce compliance if an issue arose. It took several years before all the credit union Networking Arrangements moved from the CUSOs to the credit unions but move they did. NCUA issued a letter to me from NCUA General Counsel's Office (<u>NCUA GCO Number 02-0277 dated May 24, 2002</u>) which confirmed that credit unions and not CUSOs are the proper parties in Networking Agreements. The NCUA also confirmed that credit unions may use Dual Employees to provide investment services in Networking

Arrangements (NCUA GCO Number 01-0742 dated August 31, 2001).

Non-Member Business

As CUSOs can serve non-members if CUSO's member base is primarily credit union members, CUSOs can receive commissions for non-member transactions. Now that credit unions are the parties to Networking Agreements and rely upon Incidental Powers for the authority to receive commissions, a credit union can only receive a share of commissions for member transactions. A credit union cannot be paid for non-member transactions. There is an NCUA General Counsel Opinion that confirms that position in a Networking Arrangement (NCUA GCO Number 03-0736 dated January 19, 2005). Credit unions were concerned with this complete prohibition on non-member income as an Investment Representative will often have accounts from family and friends who cannot qualify for membership in the credit union. In response to the concern, NCUA issued a draft of an Interpretive Ruling and Policy Statement ("IRPS") in 2005 ("IRPS 05-1") for comment. IRPS 05-1 was never finalized but it did provide guidance on what might be considered *de minimus* income from non-member business that would be permissible for a credit union to accept. If the income from non-member business and expenses paid for non-member business does not exceed 5% of the income and expenses for the entire Program, the credit unions could keep the non-member commission income. While never officially enacted, IRPS 05-1 has served as an informal safe harbor. Note that the member versus non-member income is not an issue for the Broker/Dealer. It is only an issue for credit unions. NCUA does not have the power under the Federal Credit Union Act to expand the Incidental Powers Regulation to include non-member income so we are left with this unofficial *de minimus* guidance.

Dual Employee Plans

There are two types of Networking Arrangements: Dual Employee Plans and Managed Plans. The difference is who pays the Investment Representative. The <u>Chubb Letter</u> specifically addressed Dual Employee Plans. The Broker/Dealer must exclusively supervise the Investment Representative when acting in that capacity which is typically full time. The credit union is responsible to oversee the Dual Employee's compliance with its employment policies such as non-discrimination and non-sexual harassment policies.

The Broker/Dealer pays the credit union a commission share and from that share, the credit union pays the Investment Representative his/her commission. The commission share to credit unions for Dual Employee Plans is typically between 80% and 92% of the GDC. The Investment Representative's portion is between 25% and 45%. The commissions paid to the credit union by the Broker/Dealer and the commissions paid to the Investment Representative by the credit union are typically scaled on a grid. The more commissions earned, the more of a percentage is paid. Depending on the size of an Investment Representative's book of business, a grid for one Investment Representative may be different from another Investment Representative.

An Investment Representative may be referred to as a Platform Representative. They are credit union employees, often branch managers, who have separate credit union duties. A Platform Representative usually has a Series 6 license and therefore can only sell mutual funds, variable annuities (if they also hold a life insurance license) and unit investment trusts. Platform Representatives can increase the members served. Due to the fact they perform credit union duties, there is a greater potential risk of a member misunderstanding that the investment products are not NCUA insured despite the disclosures made.

Managed Plans

The other type of Program is called a Managed Plan where the Investment Representative is paid by the Broker/Dealer as an employee or an independent contractor. The revenue share to the credit union ranges from 10% to 35% depending on the amount of GDC. The advantage to the credit union is the lower costs and financial risk. However, the level of impact and success tends to be lower with Managed Plans.

Networking Agreements

The following are terms that, in my experience are must-haves in the Financial Services Agreement with the Broker/Dealer to protect the credit union. Below are standard and customary contract terms that you can expect.

Term

Some Broker/Dealers will ask for a commitment to a five-year initial term. I push for a maximum of a three-year initial term with one-year renewal terms. Three years is more than sufficient time for a Broker/Dealer to recover its set-up costs and for the credit union to see if the Program is successful, but not too long in the event there is dissatisfaction in the relationship for any reason. Shorter terms resolve many contract issues.

Some Broker/Dealers try to charge an early termination fee if the credit union terminates during a term; yet another reason not to have a long term. I have resisted this contract term and most of the time it has been dropped by the Broker/Dealer. However, if a credit union does agree to it, I strongly urge that it only applies in the initial term and limit the fee to the true net income that would have been earned by the Broker/Dealer over the balance of the initial term (gross revenue to the Broker/Dealer based on averages demonstrated by the Program less anticipate expenses to service the Program) reduced to present value. This limitation makes the fee more of a reimbursement of expected revenue to offset set-up costs and less of a penalty fee.

Define the Scope of Costs

Beware of Broker/Dealers that pay a high percentage of GDC to the credit union but fees the credit union to death. A credit union must fully understand specifically what costs will be assessed during the agreement and after termination. A credit union cannot have fuzzy definitions of the costs to be reimbursed and be at the mercy of the Broker/Dealer to unilaterally determine what costs to charge. The Networking Agreement should define what costs are legitimately related to the Program and not include costs that are part of the Broker/Dealer's overhead and general compliance costs.

The cost of paying a Registered Principal needs to be negotiated. In Programs with five or six producing Investment Representatives, a Program can usually afford to pay a non-producing Registered Principal Dual Employee. In smaller Programs, the Broker/Dealer supplies the Registered Principal off-site. The usual fee for the Broker/Dealer to supply the OSJ Services through its Registered Principal is a reduction in the GDC paid to the credit union. This reduction can run between 2% to 5% of the GDC.

Member Relationship Protection

Credit unions want to protect their member relationship. The Broker/Dealer should renounce a proprietary interest in the member accounts and agree not solicit the accounts post termination. Of course, if a member desires to stay with the

Broker/Dealer without the Broker/Dealer's solicitation, that is the member's choice which should not be opposed by the credit union. Note that if there is a delay in transferring an account, the Broker/Dealer has a regulatory requirement to service the customer which may be stated in the contract. I recommend a term that states if an Investment Representative licensed with the Broker/Dealer is violating the non-solicitation and the Broker/Dealer knows about it, the Broker/Dealer agrees to take action to stop it. In order to respond to a Broker/Dealer's concern that it cannot police all the communications by an Investment Representative, the obligation arises only if the Broker/Dealer has been made aware of the improper solicitation, usually by the credit union.

Limited Exclusivity

It is fair for the Broker/Dealer to have an exclusivity clause whereby the credit union may not have a Networking Agreement for similar services with another Broker/Dealer during the term of the agreement. This exclusivity needs to be limited to securities and annuities. It should not attempt to cover insurance products other than annuities as credit unions have alternative insurance service options that can be much more effective and perhaps more profitable.

In my opinion, it is unreasonable to require exclusivity for on-line self-directed services options for the sale of securities. Credit unions need to have the ability to find the best of breed for those services if they want to offer them. This is not the strong suit for traditional Broker/Dealers. Frankly, there may not be a value-add member benefit the credit union can provide to compete against the online competitors.

Some Broker/Dealers permit credit unions the option of finding alternative fixed annuities providers and alternative

Advisory Services. Those options may be desired by some credit unions but not an absolute must-have for most credit unions.

Effective Reports

Credit unions need to receive reports from the Broker/Dealer on the investment services so the credit union can understand a members' complete financial picture. The sharing of the reports is typically permitted by the privacy rules.

Fair Indemnification and Insurance

Each party should agree to indemnify the other for liability caused by the party. The Broker/Dealer's indemnification needs to cover any and all liability created by the Investment Representatives when acting in that capacity as the Broker/Dealer exclusively supervises the Investment Representatives. There should be no damage limitations. The Broker/Dealer should have insurance for its acts and the Investment Representatives should be required to have insurance to cover their acts. Often the credit union pays the insurance premiums for the Investment Representatives for policies obtained through the Broker/Dealer's carrier. While a credit union may elect to charge the Investment Representative for the cost or portion of the cost of the insurance, most credit unions do not.

Customary Privacy Terms

The regulators and/or best practices will require that the standard privacy terms be in the agreement: (1) use information only for the Program use, (2) not disclose information outside of the Program without permission by the disclosing party unless allowed by law, (3) agree to follow the privacy laws, (4) protect the information with commercially reasonable means, (5) permit the review of the privacy protections by the other party, (6) provide notice of any breach and a promise to assist the other party to mitigate damages, and (7) return or destroy the disclosed credit union confidential information excluding data that (i) resides on customary backup, disaster recovery or business continuity systems, and (ii) is required to be maintained per applicable regulations; provided that the information retained is subject to ongoing confidentiality requirements and privacy regulations. The requirement to return or destroy information does not apply to information provided directly by the member to the Broker/Dealer.

Brand Usage
    The parties need to be comfortable in how the credit union's brand will be incorporated in the Program's marketing so that it is recognized but does not violate applicable rules such as the Chubb Letter, the NCUA, FINRA and state rules or regulations which require no ambiguity as to the fact that the Broker/Dealer is providing the services. There have been several states that have determined that the branding of the investment services has led to consumer confusion as to whether the credit union or the Broker/Dealer is providing the investment services. Large fines have been imposed upon Broker/Dealers. Both credit unions and Broker/Dealers need to understand what co-branding rules, if any, are applicable in the states of operation.

Fair Termination Practices
    The costs upon termination of the agreement can be a shock to some credit unions. I recommend having a term that limits the costs assessed to third party charges only and the Broker/Dealer is prohibited from assessing its internal costs in transition to avoid the temptation of piling on costs as the Broker/Dealer goes out the door.

    Beware that there have been instances where a

Broker/Dealer has attempted to hide customers/members accounts from the credit union by either transferring the accounts to another representative number of an Investment Representative or by transferring the accounts to another Investment Representative not associated with the credit union's Program.

There is usually a period of time after termination that is needed to transfer the accounts to the new Broker/Dealer. During that time period it is customary to continue to pay the credit union a share of trailing commissions (commissions earned prior to termination but not paid until after termination). I try to negotiate a sixty or ninety day transition period where trailing commissions are paid. If the accounts are not moved within the transition time period, the Broker/Dealer will continue to serve the accounts. However, you should have a term that states if the business has not been moved due to a delay outside of the control of the credit union or its new Broker/Dealer, the transition period will be extended.

A very big issue is whether the accounts can be transferred in bulk or whether the accounts must be signed over by the customer one account at a time. FINRA permits bulk transfer of accounts held at a Broker/Dealer for a financial institution Program but not for independent Programs. Bulk transfers for direct mutual fund and annuity accounts can be done with a negative consent notice mailing to the customers. However, there is a minimum number of accounts required for accounts held through a brokerage platform (tape-to-tape conversion) and these accounts may have to be transferred with positive consents from each customer if the minimum is not met. Bulk transfers and tape-to-tape conversion obligations should be negotiated up-front as there is no incentive for the Broker/Dealer to agree to it as accounts go out the door.

Investment Representative Agreements

It is highly recommended that the credit union have an employment agreement with the Investment Representative who is a Dual Employee. The agreement should cover the following:

- The Investment Representatives do not own the book of business they serve and that should be acknowledged by them. They should agree not to solicit any customers served after termination of employment.

- The Agreement should give the credit union the right to enforce the non-solicitation terms and the privacy terms through injunction actions. The member information should be acknowledged as a trade secret of the credit union which can give credit unions a stronger position to enforce non-solicitation terms.

- The member information should only be used for the credit union's investment services Program and not otherwise disclosed. The member information should not be taken by the Investment Representative after the Investment Representative ceases to work in the credit union's Program unless a particular member asks the Investment Representative to continue to serve him or her.

- If the Investment Representative had a book of business he or she brought to the credit union Program (usually friends and family), the credit union usually elects to allow the Investment Representative to list the accounts that will not be subject to the non-solicitation terms.

- The employment relationship is at-will and can be terminated at any time with or without cause.

- In order to avoid Department of Labor overtime issues, some credit unions pay a portion of the compensation as salary or a forgivable draw and the rest is paid in earned commissions.

- The commissions paid should be on a grid that provides tiers which reward an Investment Representative with a higher percentage of payouts as the Investment Representative earns more GDC for the credit union Program. Investment representatives with a larger book of business will tend to have higher grid percentages than new Investment Representatives. The commission percentages paid to the Investment Representative in a Dual Employee Program is less than the payout to independent Investment Representatives not in a credit union Program. The basis for the difference is that the Dual Employee Investment Representative does not have to pay for rent, computers, furniture, continuing education, licensing fees, health insurance, rental insurance, professional errors and omission insurance, and salaries for clerical and licensed assistance support. The credit union typically pays for all those costs. In addition, the credit union sends the Investment Representative a stream of warm leads which reduces the time and costs of marketing. The Dual Employee Investment Representative has a very good deal compared to his or her independent colleagues. Note that per the SEC Chubb No Action Letter, the Broker/Dealer must approve the compensation arrangement for Investment Representatives so that compensation does not provide inappropriate incentives that work against the best interest of the customers. Thus, credit unions may provide input on the payout but must obtain the Broker/Dealer's approval.

- Credit unions usually provide credit union employee benefits to the Investment Representative and, if that is the case, it should be stated in the agreement.

- If there is understanding as to when the credit union will employ a Licensed Assistant to help the Investment Representative, it should be clear that this is not a right and an assistant will be provided only if the Investment Representative maintains a minimum level of GDC production.

- Some credit unions have provisions on what will occur if the Investment Representative dies, is disabled or retires with some form of payout through the sharing of commissions with the Investment Representative that takes over the accounts for a period of time or by a fixed sum calculated based on the size of the book of business. This encourages and rewards Investment Representatives to stay with the credit union's Program and discourages Investment Representatives from trying to take the book of business and sell it to another Broker/Dealer. Note, that in order for the credit union not to lose money, the successor Investment Representative will take less in commissions to offset the credit union's payment obligations to the former Investment Representative. The goal is to make these transition payments without reducing the revenue retained by the credit union. Note also that the successor Investment Representative is not buying the book of business but rather is buying the right to serve the book of business provided he or she is doing so professionally. The agreement should be clear on that point.

I also recommend that the credit union have an agreement with the Investment Representatives in Managed Plans where there is no employment relationship the Investment Representative. The consideration is that the credit union is giving the Investment Representative access to it members. The Investment Representative should agree that the member information is confidential and will only be used in the credit union investment Program. The member information should be acknowledged as a credit union proprietary trade secret. The Investment Representative acknowledges that he or she does not own the book of business and cannot solicit the business away from the credit union's Program.

Let us consider the practical issues of solicitation of customers by Investment Representatives after they leave the credit union. The classic move is to slip a resignation letter under the door of the investment services Program Manager late on a Friday afternoon and the Investment Representative spends all weekend calling his or her key customers and asks them to sign forms to transfer their accounts to the Investment Representative's new Broker/Dealer. The fact is you cannot do much to prevent the transfer of the accounts if the customer wants to transfer. If the Investment Representative is smart and there is not a paper trail to prove the improper solicitation the credit union may have to ask its members to execute an affidavit or testify in court to prove that the Investment Representative initiated contact with the customer for the purpose of soliciting their transfer. Who wants to put members through that ordeal? The Investment Representative has usually developed a strong personal or professional relationship with the customer/member and the credit union is not going to be able to force the member to change Investment Representatives nor should they attempt anything other than gentle persuasion with the member.

Although the Broker/Dealer may assist the credit union when pursuing a violation of a non-solicitation clause, the credit union must take the lead as the credit union has the most to lose. The credit union owns the right to solicit the accounts post-termination through the Networking Agreement and is the one at risk of losing assets in the Program. If the credit union decides to enforce the terms of the contract and has strong evidence to show that the Investment Representative violated the non-solicitation clause, the credit union can usually obtain a temporary court order preventing further solicitations. Where solicitations already occurred and are proven to cause a financial loss, the credit union may be awarded monetary damages. More importantly, the credit union sends a message to the other Investment Representatives that they should be prepared to spend money on attorney fees, and court costs, plus potential damages, if they are thinking about "stealing" the credit union's members.

The best defense against the solicitation is to be ready to engage in aggressive counter solicitation as soon as the credit union becomes aware of an Investment Representative's departure. Get on the phone immediately, just like in the *Jerry Maguire* movie, and call the members served by the departing Investment Representative to assure them you have a capable replacement Investment Representative able to step in and serve them. Set up appointments to have them meet their new Investment Representative. Assign responsibility for making the calls and practice this drill so that you are ready to act immediately. Time is of the essence to prevent the departure of as many accounts as possible. Credit unions that have experienced improper solicitations have reported that they can prevent the transfer of many accounts if they act quickly, and of those accounts that do transfer, many come back over time.

Protocol Agreement

You should know about the securities industry <u>Protocol Agreement</u>. Large investment firms constantly recruit successful Investment Representatives from other firms. Most Investment Representatives are subject to non-solicitation terms which are standard and customary in the securities industry. When there is a breach or suspected breach of the non-solicitation clause, the time spent, costs, and legal fees to enforce the terms can be significant. As a result, Broker/Dealers decided to establish a protocol of how an Investment Representative can move from one Broker/Dealer to another without using deceptive tactics. Specifically, if an Investment Representative wants to move to another Broker/Dealer, they agree not to solicit customers *before* the move (it is questionable whether this is followed for the significant customers). Once notice is given, the Investment Representative will be provided a list of his or her customers (like he or she would not have the list already) and both the Investment Representative and the existing Broker/Dealer can solicit the customers and let the "best man win."

Not all Broker/Dealers are members of the <u>Protocol Agreement</u>. The <u>Protocol Agreement</u> only applies if both the Broker/Dealers involved are signatories to the <u>Protocol Agreement</u>. If the Broker/Dealer that is chosen by the credit union is a party to the <u>Protocol Agreement</u>, it is especially important in the credit union's agreement with the Investment Representative for the Investment Representative to acknowledge that the credit union is not a party to or bound by the <u>Protocol Agreement</u> and the credit union has the right to enforce the non-solicitation terms to fullest extent of the law.

Recruiting Investment Representatives

The responsibility for recruiting Investment Representatives for larger credit union Dual Employee Programs often falls upon the credit union. The credit union locates candidates through networking or classified ads and presents the candidates to the Broker/Dealer for approval. Some Broker/Dealers will actively engage in searches, but this is usually on a fee basis for a Dual Employee Program. In a Managed Plan, the Broker/Dealer supplies the Investment Representatives. Broker/Dealers will generally permit credit unions to have a veto power over the choices made by the Broker/Dealer.

FINRA maintains records on Registered Representatives. The online profile reflects the Investment Representative's past employment, licensing, and disclosures re: customer complaints and/or regulatory actions, if any. Credit Unions should review the Registered Representative's online FINRA Broker Check profile.

Success Indicators and Metrics

The most successful investment services Programs treat the securities services as part of their core offerings and just as important as any mortgage or car loan. If that level of commitment is communicated to the staff, they understand its importance to both the members and the credit union.

Having a Program Manager is also a key to success. While there are very effective and successful Program Managers who do not hold a securities license, it is a best practice to have someone run the Program who has securities industry experience. In some cases, a licensed Program Manager may also be the Registered Principal for the Program. The Program Manager interacts with the Investment Representatives and the key support people at the credit union, such as the marketing staff. The Program Manager participates in the development of a business plan, sets goals (e.g., number of qualified referrals and number of member appointments) and manages people to accomplish the goals. Without a Program Manager, the investment services are adrift and not focused. There are CUSOs that provide Program management services to multiple credit unions. The aggregation of costs and expertise through these CUSOs have helped credit unions maximize the impact of their investment Programs. The two leading CUSOs providing this service are Credit Union Financial Network, LLC and Gateway Services Group, LLC.

The absolute essential to a successful Program is to have Investment Representatives who can connect personally to the members and the credit union staff, project knowledge and confidence in their investment advice, timely follow through on commitments, and close sales without a prolonged decision-making process. A Program can be successful with great Investment Representatives and a mediocre Broker/Dealer but not vice versa. It is important that the credit union staff have confidence in the ability of the Investment Representatives to serve the members well because without that confidence, referrals will suffer.

The highest performing Programs tend to be Dual Employee Programs. There are probably several factors at work here. First is the Dual Employee Programs tend to be at larger credit unions that have the time and resources to promote the investment services. The Dual Employee is a credit union employee, a credit union team member and not an outsider which leads to more referrals. The Dual Employee feels more a part of the team with a future to encourage efforts to grow his or her book of business. There tends to be more upside income opportunities for the credit union in a Dual Employee Program than a Managed Plan due to the larger scale, performance, revenue sharing levels and commitment from the credit union.

Another success indicator is working with a Broker/Dealer who understands how to work with financial institutions, preferably credit unions. Those Broker/Dealers without such experience do not understand key elements of the relationship; i.e., the norms for commission referrals, the credit union's proprietary interests in the book of business, the privacy rules between the credit union and the Broker/Dealer, the disclosure rules and the non-solicitation terms. Non-experienced Broker/Dealers do not understand the unique ways Broker/Dealers work with financial institutions to deliver services and ensure compliance. So, the local Broker/Dealer may have nice guys who are Investment Representatives but that does not mean they will make the best partner with the credit union.

Competition for experienced Investment Representatives remains intense. The Program will need to develop strategies in the areas of talent management, recruitment and retention of experienced Investment Representatives. According to a recent industry survey, the cost of losing an experienced Investment Representative to a competitor is around $2 million, even if they do not take customers or assets with them.

The number of Investment Representatives in a Program is approximately one (1) Investment Representative per $100M to $150M in credit union assets. The credit union will need to perform an analysis of the deposit assets in each territory and have a strategy to service member accounts with investable assets of less than $100,000. Investable assets in accounts that have less than $100,000 will not generate the GDC required to support bottom line results in the long-term and will affect the Program's ability to retain experienced Investment Representatives. Developing a customer service model focused on varying levels of service based on revenue generated is one approach that can be taken to address the account profitability factor. In other words, service levels based on customer needs, expectations and assets under management. Customers with lower amounts in their portfolio may be served by less experienced Investment Representatives or Platform Representatives if services can be delivered in a competent manner.

The shift from transactional business to managed or "fee based advisory accounts" for most credit unions has changed the dynamics of what is considered a well-performing Investment Representative. Recent studies of credit unions' investment Programs indicate that an experienced producing Investment Representative should average over $30,000 in GDC per month. It should take a new Investment Representative starting with a nominal book of business three to four years to reach this level of productivity. It is important to note that there is continued downward pressure on fee-based revenue with the advent of low-cost investment options such as exchange traded fund providers and digital options, including Robo trading.

A metric that should be considered is the number of new assets under management ("AUM") that the Investment Representative is bringing on board each month. For a new Investment Representative in the first year of production, a realistic goal is to produce $500,000 to $750,000 per month in new AUM ($6M - $9M annually). The average in 2016 was $7.2 million. For an experienced tenured Investment Representative, a goal of $1 million per month is reasonable ($12 million annually).

Before a credit union can afford to pay a full time non-producing Program Manager/Registered Principal, the Program should have five to six producing Investment Representatives. The commissions paid to Investment Representatives range from 25% to 45% (for very high producers). The average is 38%. The number of customers and the assets under management should be the primary drivers in deciding when a Licensed Assistant is hired to assist an Investment Representative. A good rule of thumb is that the AUM should be greater than $30 million with approximately 400 customers. It is important to note that a Licensed Assistant is different from administrative support (non-Licensed Assistant). Commissions cannot be shared with non-licensed individuals, but a bonus structure based on production and asset acquisition can be established with a Licensed Assistant. A Licensed Assistant can be one strategy in the servicing of some of the smaller accounts (accounts with AUM less than $100,000) and will allow the experienced Investment Representative to continue to grow AUM while meeting customer service standards. Investment Representatives should be averaging GDC production of at least $30,000 per month before a dedicated Licensed Assistant is hired to help the Investment Representative

The annual cost for an Investment Representative's licenses, professional liability insurance and continuing education is approximately $9,500 (this amount could be higher if the Investment Representative has customers in several States) and will require additional expenses of approximately $5,000 if assigned a Licensed Assistant. A Program with five to six producing Investment Representatives generally will have one Licensed Assistant that is shared by the group and one non-licensed administrative support that is shared by the group.

An investment services penetration of over 2% of the credit union membership is at the higher end of credit union

Programs. Do not neglect to measure the number of credit union products used by the investment members versus other members. If the studies show that the members using investment services use more credit union services, that is an added benefit of the Program.

CHAPTER 3
INSURANCE SERVICES

Why Provide Insurance Services?

The answer is to make additional income and provide a needed member service. Some insurance products complement lending services, i.e., title insurance, and property and casualty insurance. If the credit union staff is motivated to refer borrowers to the credit union's insurance provider when the need for insurance is presented to the borrower in the lending process, it is a convenience to the member and an income opportunity to the credit union. Of course, in consumer transactions you cannot condition the loan approval or loan terms on buying insurance from the credit union's insurance provider.

Typically, the sale of annuities is made by the Investment Representatives in the investment Program and all other insurance products are sold by other means, e.g., group life, long term care, accidental death and disability, title, GAP, and health.

How Insurance Services are Offered?

Pure Referral Model

The easiest way for a credit union to sell insurance products to members is to contract with an Insurance Agency to sell to its members. Insurance Agencies with a large credit union customer base include CUNA Mutual, Allied Solutions and Gateway Services Group. The credit union provides its membership list, cooperation in co-marketing and endorsement. The credit union is paid a small share of commissions. There is lower revenue from this model but also lower risks and costs.

Build It from Scratch Model

Sometimes a credit union decides it wants to form a CUSO and build an agency from scratch. If tried by the credit union on its own, it seldom turns out well. In order to be successful, the CUSO will have to convince the Insurance Carriers to appoint the CUSO as an agency to sell their products. The Insurance Carriers are very selective on whom they appoint and if a CUSO has no insurance history or customers, the CUSO is not going to get the desired appointments. Actual customers, not potential customers, matter to the Insurance Carriers because it costs them money to open and manage agency relationships.

There is a company that uses scale to overcome the appointment issues in the start-up model. Insuritas has negotiated with Insurance Carriers to appoint Insuritas' CUSO customers as agents. The pitch to the Insurance Carriers being the business volume will come through this aggregated effort. Insuritas charges an upfront fee and shares commissions with the credit union's CUSO.

Agency Purchase Model

Credit unions have had success buying local Insurance Agencies. Local Insurance Agencies have exiting carrier appointments, an existing customer base that generates revenue, and an experienced staff. Typically, the owners of the agency are near retirement and are looking for a liquidation event. The owners are usually paid over time with an earn-out provision that pays more if the amount of business remains the same or increases over the payout period. The owners remain as employees with employment agreements during the payout period. The sale is usually a stock sale so that the carrier appointments and licenses remain in place. If unknown liabilities arise post-closing, the amounts can be deducted from the payout obligation. The challenge is that the Insurance Agency, now a CUSO when the credit union buys it, will not primarily serve credit union members at the point of purchase which puts the CUSO out of compliance with the CUSO rules. Thus, the CUSO must work hard to meet the customer base requirement by (a) signing up insurance customers as members if possible and (b) by marketing insurance services to the members. There is no official grace period regarding non- compliance with the primarily serves rule, but credit union regulators will not normally raise this as an issue if you have a plan to come into compliance in the short term. The advantages of buying an Insurance Agency is that the CUSO will own the book of business, share in the full agency commissions, and have full control of the agency relationship with the customer/member. I recommend that credit unions use experts on the valuation of the shares as you do not want to overpay.

Partner Model

In this model the credit union partners with an Insurance Agency in a CUSO. The CUSO is an Insurance Agency that is co-owned by the credit union and partner Insurance Agency ("Partner Agency"). This is a common model for title insurance agencies where the Partner Agency's personnel are hired by the CUSO to provide the title insurance services and the profits are split between the credit union and the Partner Agency.

The partner model is sometimes used for property and casualty insurance but my experience is that the relationship does not last long. The Partner Agency makes less money in the CUSO relationship and is less motivated to spend resources on the CUSO versus the Partner Agency's own separate business. Sometimes it is the credit union that disappoints the expectations of the Partner Agency by not sending as many referrals as expected by the Partner Agency.

The Rules

The states and not the federal government regulate the insurance industry. There is no Chubb Letter-like license exemption in the insurance industry. If a person or entity wants to share insurance commissions, it must have the proper state insurance license. In most states this means that the Insurance Agency entity must have a person with a broker license associate his or her license with the entity and then the entity must obtain an entity license. Note that in some states a person does not have to be employed by the Insurance Agency in order to associate his or her license with the Insurance Agency and the person can associate his or her license with multiple Insurance Agencies.

NCUA confirmed in 2001 that a credit union could

receive insurance commission income from an Insurance Agency selling to its members, provided that the credit union complies with state insurance laws which includes obtaining an agency license. NCUA General Counsel's Office (NCUA GCO Number 01-0869 dated November 14, 2001). A credit union does not have the power to perform any function of an insurance agency and only receives a license in order to legally accept commissions. If a credit union wants to operate a fully functioning Insurance Agency, it needs to form a CUSO and have the CUSO obtain the Insurance Agency license. Note, that if the CUSO is licensed and is paid a share of commissions, the credit union, as an owner, can receive its ownership dividends from the CUSO without being licensed.

The insurance commission model differs depending on the product. All commission structures are registered and approved by the state insurance commission. The state insurance commission rules that apply are from the state where the customer resides.

Title Insurance
To receive insurance commissions as a title Insurance Agency, a CUSO must be used. The Real Estate Settlement and Procedures Act ("RESPA") prevents referral commissions to be paid to the credit union. Title insurance commissions are particularly lucrative for agencies. The amount of the premium for the title insurance from Insurance Carrier ranges from 10% to 15%, while the agency receives the balance of the premiums as commissions. Title agency CUSOs tend to be joint ventures that are co-owned by one credit union and an experienced title agency. However, some larger credit unions have hired experienced title agents and have started an agency from scratch either solely owning the title agency CUSO or being a majority owner with the title agent having a minority equity position.

RESPA requires that profits can only be shared proportionate to the cash investment made by the owners. So, having more than one credit union as an owner tends to be problematic as profits cannot be shared based on the source of the business. The CUSO title agency must assume the normal business risks of a title Insurance Agency and have employees. The CUSO cannot be a shell of an organization. In practical terms this means the CUSO must be generating revenue in excess of $100,000 per year in order to afford the costs of running an independent agency. This should not be a problem for the larger credit unions but will keep smaller credit unions out of the title agency insurance business. In some states, a title Insurance Agency must be associated with a title plant which is a business that owns and maintains real estate records. In those states the cost of a title plant makes owning a small title Insurance Agency cost prohibitive.

<u>Property and Casualty</u>

There are up front commissions paid to agents and a back end or experienced based commissions that are paid annually depending on whether the number of claims from the book of business was within or exceeded the projections. The P & C business is very competitive, and the margins are small. However, over time, and with good experience-based commissions, there are profits to be made. In the perfect world, an agency will have a balance of both consumer and commercial business.

If a referral is made in a lending situation, there is a disclosure called an affiliate business arrangement disclosure that must be given. This discloses the fact that the credit union lender has an ownership interest or fee sharing relationship with the insurance service provider but does not disclose the details of the business relationship. Understand that you cannot condition the approval of a loan or the loan terms upon whether the member buys insurance.

Accidental Death and Disability

This insurance requires an agreement with the credit union stay in place for a specified time period after a member solicitation is mailed and usually multiple solicitations are made. This can and has resulted in an evergreen effect where a credit union feels trapped and can never seem to end a relationship. But do not feel bad for the credit unions. They usually get a very big advanced commission payment up front. Note that there are privacy issues that must be managed. In the solicitation of the product, you have to be careful not to provide the member information to the AD&D insurance provider but rather to a third party marketer hired by the credit union (but usually paid by insurance provider). Otherwise, there are privacy opt-out notices and rights that would have to be given.

Commission Sharing Agreements

In joint marketing agreements with third party Insurance Agencies the following are terms that, in my experience, are must-haves.

Term

The insurance provider needs sufficient time initially to complete a marketing cycle but after that period of time, the credit union should have the ability to terminate the agreement upon thirty or sixty days' notice. Note, the AD&D termination issue discussed above and make sure there is a practical way to end the relationship.

Define the Scope of Costs

Make sure the credit union is very clear on whether there are costs involved and the definition of the duties of the credit union. For example, sometimes credit unions are surprised that they agreed to a certain level of marketing duties in the agreement.

Member Relationship Protection

Credit unions want to protect the member relationship so there should be a term in the agreement that prevents the insurance provider from soliciting members post-termination of the agreement. Sometimes an insurance provider will want a credit union to refrain from soliciting members to move insurance products away from them post-termination. I would not agree to this term, but some credit unions have agreed not to solicit current customers until their respective policies come up for renewal. If the credit union agrees to this limited non-solicitation period, I would ask to continue commission sharing on the policies not being solicited.

Limited Exclusivity

It is fair to require that the credit union not work with another provider selling the same product during the term of the agreement but make sure the exclusivity is precisely defined so that you are not unnecessarily reducing your options.

Effective Reports

Credit unions need to receive reports from the insurance providers on the business written so the credit union can understand a members' complete financial picture. The sharing of the reports is permitted by the privacy rules without an opt-out clause if the Insurance Agency's privacy policy and privacy policy so states.

Fair Indemnification and Insurance

    Each party should agree to indemnify the other for liability caused by the party. There should be no damage limitations. The insurance provider should have professional liability insurance for its negligent acts.

Customary Privacy Terms

    The regulators and/or best practices will require that the standard privacy terms be in the agreement: (1) use information only for the Program use, (2) not disclose information outside the Program without permission by the disclosing party unless allowed by law, (3) agree to follow the privacy laws, (4) protect the information with commercially reasonable means but, in any event not less than the party protects its confidential information, (5) permit the review of the privacy protections by the other party, (6) provide notice of any breach and a promise to assist the other party to mitigate damages, and (7) return or destroy the disclosed confidential information excluding data that (i) resides on customary backup, disaster recovery or business continuity systems, and (ii) is required to be maintained per applicable regulations provided that the information retained is subject to ongoing confidentiality requirements and privacy regulations. Note that the credit union's privacy protection terms do not apply to information provided directly by the member to the third-party Insurance Agency. Note that the Fair and Accurate Credit Transactions Act prevents the sharing of any information used to analyze the creditworthiness of the member without an opt-out clause.

Brand Usage

    The parties need to be comfortable in how the credit union's brand will be incorporated in the Program's marketing so that it is recognized but does not violate applicable insurance laws.

Direct Relationships with Insurance Carriers

If a CUSO is an Insurance Agency with direct contractual relationships with Insurance Carriers, the CUSO has no bargaining power to alter terms. That is not to say the agreements will be unfair but that is the reality of the situation.

Success Indicators

Credit unions that appoint a person to oversee the relationship with the third-party Insurance Agency partners tend to have higher performance with the sale of insurance. The Program Managers for insurance services work with credit union staff and the Insurance Agencies to maximize referrals and provide education on the member benefits. The Program Manager is often a licensed Insurance Agent.

Marketing is important. Members have to know the service is available before they ask for it. Referrals from credit union employees are crucial. However, even if referrals are made too many credit unions let leads die on the vine. Some credit unions pay nominal referral fees to staff to maximize referrals. If so, the credit union or CUSO should research the state's insurance laws to confirm the scope of what it legal to pay in the state. If a state permits referral fees to be paid to unlicensed persons, the referral fees cannot be contingent upon the sale of an insurance product.

If the credit union pays attention to the referral rates, the speed to contact the referrals and the closing rates, the credit union will be measuring the right metrics to achieve success. Financial returns take longer in insurance services than in investment services. The margins are smaller for most insurance products and the commissions on sales can be modest. However, a lot of small commissions over time can provide a significant alternative revenue stream to the credit union. By providing a convenient and valuable service to your members, credit unions are helping to meet the financial needs of its members.

CHAPETER $
APPENDIX

SEC Chubb Letter	53
NCUA Letter 10-FCU-03	65
FINRA 3160	81
NCUA Incidental Powers	87
NCUA GCO 02-0277	89
NCUA GCO 01-0742	93
NCUA GCO 03-0736	97
NCUA IRPS 05-1	101
Protocol for Broker Recruiting	105
NCUA GCO 01-0869	111

Securities and Exchange Commission

November 24, 1993

Ian E. Celecia, Esq.
Chubb Securities Corporation One Granite Place
P.O. Box 2005
Concord, New Hampshire 03302

Re: Chubb Securities Corporation

Dear Mr. Celecia:

In your letter of September 1, 1993, on behalf of Chubb Securities Corporation ("CSC"), as supplemented by telephone conversations with the staff, you request assurance that the staff would not recommend enforcement action to the Commission under Section 15(a)(1) of the Securities Exchange Act of 1934 ("Exchange Act") if CSC enters into networking arrangements with certain federal and state chartered banks, savings and loan associations, savings banks, and credit unions (collectively, "Financial Institutions") and, where required by law, their service corporation subsidiaries, to provide securities brokerage services on the premises of such Financial Institutions, as described in your letter, without the Financial Institutions, the required service corporations, or their unregistered employees registering as broker-dealers under Section 15(b) of the Exchange Act.

We understand the facts to be as follows:

CSC, a wholly-owned subsidiary of Chubb Life Insurance Company of America, is a registered broker-dealer and member of the National Association of Securities Dealers, Inc. ("NASD"). CSC proposes to enter into networking arrangements with Financial Institutions to provide securities brokerage services to customers of such Financial Institutions and the general public, on the premises of the Financial Institutions. Where required by the laws or regulations governing a Financial Institution, the Financial Institution will enter into the networking arrangement with CSC through a service corporation subsidiary of the Financial Institution.

CSC will provide brokerage services on the premises for each Financial Institution in an area that is physically separate from the Financial Institution's regular business activities, in such a way as to clearly segregate and distinguish CSC from the Financial Institution. The area in which CSC provides brokerage services will clearly display CSC's name and an indication that CSC is a member of the NASD, and will be registered with the NASD as a branch office of CSC. Under the networking arrangements, CSC will provide brokerage services only on the premises of Financial Institutions themselves, and not in areas where a service corporation has a location independent of the Financial Institution.

The networking arrangement between CSC and each Financial Institution including its required service corporation) will be governed by a Customer Access Agreement, which will set forth the responsibilities of the parties, the conditions of the arrangement, and the compensation to be received by the Financial Institution (including its required service corporation). As a registered broker-dealer, CSC will comply with all statutory and regulatory requirements applicable to broker-dealers, including applicable rules of self-regulatory organizations ("SROs"). CSC will exclusively control, supervise, and be responsible for all securities business conducted in its locations at the Financial Institutions. Under the networking arrangements, transactions in securities may be effected only by registered representatives of CSC, some of whom also may be employees of the Financial Institution, including its required service corporation ("Dual Employees"). CSC will control, properly supervise, and responsible for all its registered representatives, including any Dual Employees acting in their capacity as CSC registered representatives.

Any materials used by CSC or the Financial Institutions (including required service corporations) to advertise or promote the availability of brokerage services under the networking arrangements will be approved by CSC for compliance with the federal securities laws prior to distribution. All such materials will be deemed to be CSC's materials, and will indicate clearly that the brokerage services are being provided by CSC and not the Financial Institution or its required service corporation; that neither the Financial Institution nor its required service corporation is a registered broker or dealer; that the customer will be dealing solely with CSC with respect to the brokerage services; and that CSC is not affiliated with the Financial Institution or its required service corporation. References to a Financial Institution in advertising or promotional materials will be for the purpose of identifying the location where brokerage services are available only, and will not appear prominently in such materials.

All confirmations, account statements, and other customer communications regarding securities transactions under the networking arrangements will be sent directly to the customer by CSC or by the issuer, transfer agent, or principal underwriter of the security. All documentation sent by CSC directly to a customer, including confirmations and account statements, will indicate clearly that the brokerage services are provided by CSC and not the Financial Institution or its required service corporation. If any documentation regarding securities transactions is sent directly to a customer of CSC by an issuer, transfer agent, or principal underwriter, CSC will be responsible for ensuring that such materials comply with the federal securities laws, and the name of the Financial Institution or its required service corporation will not appear on such materials.

Each Financial Institution (including required service corporations)will allow supervisory personnel of CSC and representatives of the Commission, the NAS and other SROs of which CSC is a member, as well as other applicable federal and state governmental authorities, to inspect the Financial Institutions premises where CSC conducts brokerage activities and any books and records maintained by CSC with respect to brokerage activities. Each Financial Institution (including required service corporations) will be deemed to be an associated person of CSC within the meaning of Section J (a)(18) of the Exchange Act.

Employees of the Financial Institution (including required service corporations) who are not registered representative of CSC will not engage in any securities or investments related activities on behalf of CSC. Unregistered employees will be prohibited from recommending any security or giving any other form of investment advice, describing investment vehicles such as mutual funds, discussing the merits of any security or giving type of security with a customer, or handling any question that might require familiarity with the securities industry or the exercise of judgment regarding securities and investment alternatives. Unregistered employees will refer all securities-related questions to registered representatives of CSC. All telephone inquiries related to CSC will be answered solely by registered representatives of CSC. Unregistered employees will be prohibited from accepting or transmitting orders, handling customer funds or securities (except that unregistered employees may effect electronic funds transfers to CSC from an account at the Financial Institution or required service corporation at a customer's request) or having any involvement in securities transactions other than providing clerical and ministerial assistance.

Unregistered employees of the Financial Institutions (including required service corporations) will not receive any compensation based on transactions in securities or the provision of securities advice. Unregistered employees may, however, be paid a nominal fee for referring Financial Institution customers to CSC. The amount of any such fees, which will be unrelated to the volume of securities traded by the customer, will be· determined and paid by the Financial Institution (or required service corporation. Unregistered employees will; be paid no more than one fee per customer referred. Other than this one-time, nominal fee, unregistered employees will not receive any other compensation, such as trips, free meals, or monetary awards, as the result of a referral or the number of referrals made. Supervisory employees will not receive any fees for referrals made by their subordinates.

    CSC will provide conduct manuals to unregistered employees of the Financial Institutions (and required service corporations) that specify the limits on their permissible activities, as set forth above. Each Financial Institution (including required service corporations) will monitor the activities of its unregistered employees, and ensure their compliance with the limits on their permissible activities as set forth in the conduct manual. Furthermore, CSC will conduct periodic reviews to assure that the Financial Institutions (including required service corporations) and their unregistered employees comply with the limits on their activities set forth in the conduct manual. CSC also will provide each of its registered representatives with a copy of CSC's compliance manual. Registered representatives will adhere to the policies and procedures contained in CSC's compliance manual. CSC will monitor its registered representatives compliance in this regard.

All brokerage services provided at the Financial Institutions (including required service corporations) will be provided by registered representatives of CSC, either Dual Employees or otherwise, all of whom will be registered and qualitied as necessary with the Commission, the NASD, and any appropriate state regulatory authorities, and all of whom will be associated persons of CSC within the meaning of Section 3(a)(18)of the Exchange Act. Each Financial Institution including required service corporations) will agree chat any Dual Employee whom the Commission, the NASD, or CSC bars or suspends from association with CSC or any other broker-dealer will be terminated or suspended, accordingly, from all securities activities by the Financial Institution (and its required service corporation). The securities activities of each Dual Employee will be supervised by the supervisory personnel of CSC, who are registered securities principals. The amount of any transaction-related compensation paid to CSC's registered representatives, including Dual Employees, under the networking arrangement, will be determined solely by CSC. For convenience with respect to tax and social security withholding, health, retirement, and other benefits, transaction-related compensation may be paid to Dual Employees by the employer Financial Institution (including required service corporations),provided that it "is clear that such payments are made on behalf of CSC from funds allocated by CSC for payment of Dual Employees.

Registered representatives are required to inform all securities customers, and obtain a written acknowledgment from such customers, that the brokerage services are being provided by CSC and not by the Financial Institution (or its required service corporation), and that the offered securities are net guaranteed by the Financial Institution (or its required service corporation) or insured by the Federal Deposit Insurance Corporation ("FDIC") or any other federal or state deposit guarantee fund relating to financial institutions.

CSC will not solicit customers of a Financial Institution in connection with the purchase or sale of the securities of that institution or any of its affiliates (including required service corporations). CSC may execute unsolicited transactions in the equity securities of the Financial Institution or its affiliates (including required service corporations) on behalf of a Financial Institution customer, provided that the customer signs an affidavit affirming that the transaction was effected on an unsolicited basis and that the customer has been informed that the securities are not insured by the Financial Institution or any of its affiliates (including required service corporations>. the FDIC, or any other state or federal deposit guarantee funds relating to financial institutions.

No debt securities of the Financial Institution or its affiliates (including its required service corporations) will be sold, on an unsolicited basis or otherwise, on any part of the premises of the Financial Institution that is generally accessible to the public.

CSC will pay a fee to the each Financial Institution (including required service corporations)based on all securities transactions that occur at or are attributable to activities conducted on that Financial Institution's premises. CSC will provide a copy of this letter to each Financial Institution (including required service corporations) and will ensure that each Financial Institution (including required service corporations) understands its obligations under the networking arrangement.

Response:
On the first of your representations and the facts presented, and strict adherence thereto by CSC, the Financial Institutions (including required

service corporations) and their unregistered employees, and particularly in view of the fact that CSC is a registered broker-dealer and all personnel engaged in securities activities under the networking arrangements will be fully subject to the regulatory requirements of the federal securities laws and the applicable rules of SROs, the staff would not recommend enforcement action to the Commission under Section 15 (a)(1)of the Exchange Act if CSC offers brokerage services under the networking arrangements described above without the Financial Institutions (including required service corporations) and their unregistered employees registering as broker-dealers under Section 15(b) of the Exchange Act. This staff position is based in part on CSC's representation that it will control, properly supervise, and be responsible for all registered representatives participating in the networking arrangements. Consequently, any designation of such registered representatives as "independent contractors" will have no effect on CSC's responsibilities under the federal securities laws, including without limitation, Sections 15 (b)and 20(a) of the Exchange Act.

This position concerns enforcement action only and does not represent a legal, conclusion regarding the applicability of the statutory or regulatory provisions of the federal securities laws. Moreover, this position is based solely on the representations that you have made; any different facts or conditions may require a different response.

Sincerely,

CatherineMcGuire
Chief Counsel

NCUA LETTER TO FEDERAL CREDIT UNION

LETTER NO.: 10-FCU-03

DATE: December 2010
TO: Federal Credit Unions
SUBJ: Sales of Nondeposit Investments

Dear Board of Directors:

The purpose of this letter is to provide guidance to federal credit unions on the establishment and operation of third party brokerage arrangements for sales of nondeposit investment products. This letter supersedes and replaces NCUA's Letter to Credit Unions No. 150 (December 1993) (Letter No. 150), which contains NCUA's previous guidance to credit unions on the sales of nondeposit investments.

NCUA needs to update its guidance because of several changes that have taken place since Letter No. 150 was issued in 1993. First, NCUA replaced the group purchasing activities rule with the incidental powers rule, eliminating some restrictions on the compensation a federal credit union may receive for its finder activities. See 12 C.F.R. Part 721. Second, the NCUA Office of General

Counsel has issued several legal opinion letters since 1993 regarding the sale of nondeposit investments that add to or refine the previous guidance.

Background

Nondeposit investments, including stocks, bonds, mutual funds, and variable annuities, are subject to a complex set of federal and state securities laws. In particular, federal securities laws require that any entity "engaged in the business of effecting transactions in securities for the account of others," must register as a securities broker with the SEC and comply with SEC broker-dealer regulations. See 15 U.S.C.78c.

Historically, banks had enjoyed a "blanket exemption" from SEC's broker-dealer registration requirements until Congress repealed this broad exemption in the Gramm-Leach-Bliley Act of 1999 (GLBA). GLBA sets out specific exemptions for certain bank activities.

The Financial Services Regulatory Relief Act of 2006 (FSRRA) required the SEC and the Federal Reserve to jointly issue a regulation governing the broker exemptions. FSRRA also amended the definition of the term "bank" to include thrifts or other savings associations insured by the Federal Deposit Insurance Corporation (FDIC). In 2007, the SEC and the Federal Reserve issued Regulation R to implement the GLBA broker exemptions relating to third party networking arrangements, trust and fiduciary activities, sweep activities, and safekeeping and custody activities. *See* 12 C.F.R. Part 218; 17 C.F.R. Parts 240 and 247; *see also* 72 Fed. Reg. 56,514 (Oct. 3, 2007). Regulation R does not apply to federal credit unions.

Federal credit unions have limited powers and are not authorized under the Federal Credit Union Act (the Act) to sell nondeposit investments directly to their members. Further, federal credit unions cannot register as broker-dealers because the SEC requirements, including capital and reserve requirements, are inconsistent with those NCUA and state supervisory authorities place on federal credit unions. Federal credit unions, therefore, must structure their securities activities carefully to strictly meet the terms of SEC guidance applicable to federal credit unions contained in a "no action" letter. *See, eg.,* Chubb Securities Corp., 1993 SEC No-Act. LEXIS 1204 (Nov. 24, 1993) (Chubb Letter).

The most common way for federal credit

unions to offer nondeposit investment products to their members is by employing third party brokerage arrangements. Federal credit unions involved in third party brokerage arrangements must have a written agreement clearly outlining the duties and responsibilities of each party in the arrangement. Generally, there are three permissible ways to structure a third party brokerage arrangement. First, a credit union may wholly or partly own a credit union service organization (CUSO) that sells nondeposit investment products, primarily to credit union members. Based on the SEC's review of the extent of the CUSO's involvement in the purchase and sale of nondeposit investment products, the CUSO may have to register with the SEC as a broker-dealer.

Second, a federal credit union may use a shared employee arrangement with a third party brokerage firm. In a shared employee arrangement, a "dual employee" operates as both a federal credit union employee and an employee of a third party broker. A shared employee may sell nondeposit investment products to the credit union's members on its premises or from another location; however, it must be clear that when a shared employee is selling nondeposit investment products, the employee is acting exclusively in his or her capacity as an employee of the third party broker, not the credit union. See OGG Op. 01-0742 (Aug. 31, 2001).

Third, a federal credit union may act as a finder. The incidental powers rule allows a federal credit union to bring, through a networking agreement or other means, a registered third party broker to its members for the sale of nondeposit investment products. 12 U.S.C. §1757; 12 C.F.R. §721.3(f). A federal credit union may earn income from finder activities. 12 C.F.R. §721.6; OGG Op. 02-0523a (May 24, 2002). The SEC permits credit unions to receive transaction-related compensation from the third party broker without triggering the broker-dealer registration requirements, as long as the brokerage arrangement adheres strictly to the terms of the Chubb Letter.

Guidelines for the Sales of Nondeposit Investments

I. Scope

The guidelines in this letter provide assistance and direction to federal credit unions offering the sale of nondeposit investment products to their members through third party brokerage arrangements, including:

- Sales by a CUSO wholly or partly owned by a federal credit union.

- Sales by a "dual employee" operating as both a credit union employee and an employee of a third party broker.

- Sales resulting from a federal credit union bringing a registered third party broker to its members through a networking agreement or other means.

II. *General Guidelines*

Federal credit unions must comply with all the applicable laws, regulations, and sound business practices in the sale of nondeposit investment products through third party brokerage arrangements. The credit union's directors should, as with any business activity, fully evaluate the risks involved with nondeposit investment activities, including legal risks, reputation risks, and economic risks.

A. Due Diligence

Federal credit unions should take care to select an appropriate broker before entering into a third party brokerage arrangement for the sale of nondeposit investment products. In selecting a third party broker, credit unions should:

- Ensure the broker can provide the

services credit union members need.

- Review the broker's financial statements and capital adequacy.
- Determine if the broker can adequately supervise its sales representatives at the credit union's location.

- Seek references for the broker and the sales representatives that will be working at the credit union (preferably other depository institutions) and speak with those references.

- Conduct background and Financial Industry Regulatory Authority (FINRA) checks on the broker's principals and the sales representatives that will be working at the federal credit union. For example, FINRA BrokerCheck® is a free resource federal credit unions can utilize to help research the professional backgrounds of current and former FINRA-registered brokerage firms and brokers.

- Retain key documentation reflecting its due diligence process in selecting a broker for a third party brokerage arrangement. Documentation should be made available to NCUA examiners, if necessary.

B.   Credit Union Policies, Procedures and Agreements

The federal credit union's board of directors should adopt written policies and procedures concerning third party brokerage arrangements to ensure compliance with applicable law and regulation and to ensure consistency with these guidelines. Credit unions should consider engaging legal counsel to evaluate their policies, procedures, and contractual agreements.

Federal credit unions must have a written agreement outlining the duties and responsibilities of each party in a third party brokerage arrangement. Contracts with third party brokers should reflect the federal credit union's policies and procedures regarding brokerage arrangements. At a minimum, the credit union's policies, procedures, and contracts should address the following:

• *The features of the sales program.* Credit union policies and agreements should describe the types of products that a broker may offer through the third party brokerage arrangement. For all products, the credit union should identify specific laws, regulations, and any other limitations or requirements, including qualitative considerations, that will expressly govern the selection and marketing of products a third party broker may offer. Qualitative considerations include an analysis of the level of complexity and volatility in the investments that the credit union will permit the broker to offer members. For example, comprehensive qualitative investment data (e.g., key ratios, dollar amounts, risk parameters, etc.) should be prepared and presented to the federal credit union's management and board of directors for review.

• *A description of the responsibilities of the credit union and the third party broker.* Credit union policies and contracts should make clear that the third party broker is primarily responsible for ensuring that the nondeposit sales function is conducted in compliance with all applicable laws, regulations, and policies. The credit union should maintain the right to check for compliance and access member accounts for verification and oversight.

• *Indemnification by the third party broker.* Credit unions should require contracts with third party brokers to include provisions to indemnify the federal credit union for any monetary damages arising from nondeposit sales activities.

- *The roles of credit union, third party broker, and dual employees.* Policies should describe the roles of credit union employees in nondeposit investment activities, including the limits on their activities. Policies and contracts should also identify and describe the duties of the broker's sales representatives and indicate who will supervise the sales representatives. If the third party brokerage arrangement involves the use of a dual employee, credit union policies should include job descriptions for the duties performed for the credit union and the nondeposit investment sales duties performed for the third party broker. Credit unions should seek an indemnification agreement from the broker, as described above, to limit credit union liability arising from employee misconduct related to nondeposit investment activities conducted by a dual employee.

- *The location of nondeposit sales.* Credit union policies should describe where nondeposit sales may take place and how those sales will be separated from deposit-taking activities.

- *The use of credit union member information.* Policies should describe the information that may be transferred between the credit union and the third party broker or the broker's sales representative. The policies and contracts should describe how such information will be used, how the information will be safeguarded, and the associated privacy notices to be provided to members. The policies and contract terms should comply with NCUA's Privacy of Consumer Financial Information Rule and NCUA's Security Program Rule. 12 C.F.R. Parts 716 and 748. The third party broker should agree in writing to comply with the credit union's policies on information practices.

• *Termination of the contract.* Contracts should contain a provision that permits the credit union to terminate the contract for both cause and for the convenience of the credit union. Failure by the third party broker to supervise its sales representative adequately should be included as a specific for-cause reason for contract termination.

• *Compliance with the requirements of all applicable law and regulation.* Credit unions should maintain programs to monitor compliance by the third party broker, its salespeople, and other entities involved in the sales of nondeposit investments. The compliance function should be performed independently of any nondeposit investment product sales and management. At a minimum, the compliance function should include a system that monitors member complaints and periodically reviews and randomly samples member account activity to look for evidence of abuse. Credit unions should also provide regular, periodic compliance reports to their board of directors to ensure appropriate oversight.

C. Conduct in Third Party Brokerage Arrangements

Federal credit unions offering the sale of nondeposit investment products through a third party brokerage arrangement should do so in a manner that does not mislead or confuse members as to the nature or risks of these uninsured products. To avoid member confusion, third party brokers should not offer investment products with a product name that is intentionally similar to the federal credit union's name.

If the third party brokerage arrangement involves the use of shared employees, the dual employee should not use any materials that could potentially confuse a member as to the capacity in which the dual employee is functioning. For example, dual employees should use separate business cards for their credit union and investment sales functions. Likewise, dual employees should use separate stationery for credit union correspondence and investment activity correspondence.

When selling, advertising, or otherwise marketing uninsured investment products to members, members must be informed that the products offered:

- are not federally-insured;

- are not obligations of the credit union;

- are not guaranteed by the credit union;

- involve investment risk; and

- if applicable, are being offered by a dual employee who accepts deposits on behalf of the credit union and also sells nondeposit investment products on behalf of a third party broker.

These disclosures should be made in writing and in a location and type size that are clear and conspicuous to the member. Oral disclosures should also be made as part of any oral sales presentation.

Credit union policies should specifically address the locations at which sales will take place. The credit union's routine deposit-taking activities should be physically separated from nondeposit investment sales functions to emphasize that important differences exist between these activities, such as the degree of risk and insurability. If limited office space makes physical separation of these functions impractical, nondeposit investment sales and deposit-taking may be conducted in close proximity to each other if appropriate disclosures, as described above, are made to members.

D. Investment Advice

No employee of a federal credit union may provide investment advice that would subject the employee or credit union to federal or state securities laws. A federal credit union, however, may offer investment advice services to its members by establishing a shared employee arrangement with a third party registered investment adviser. The dual employee may provide investment advice on behalf of the third party, but not the credit union. A federal credit union may also act as a finder to introduce or otherwise bring together an outside vendor of investment adviser services to its members or wholly or partly own a CUSO that provides investment adviser services. OGC Op. 09-0511 (June 3, 2009). A CUSO may have to register with the SEC as a Registered Investment Adviser (RIA). 15 U.S.C. §80-3(a).

III. Conclusion

Compliance with this letter is essential for credit unions to establish third party brokerage arrangements properly and prevent triggering SEC's broker-dealer registration requirements. By adhering to these guidelines, credit unions will also help to avoid member confusion about the risk and uninsured nature of nondeposit investment products. Prudent management of securities activities will ensure credit unions are offering their members nondeposit investment options in a safe and sound manner.

If you have any questions related to this letter, you should contact your regional office or district examiner.

Sincerely,

Debbie Matz,
Chairman

[footnotes have been deleted]

FINRA 3160. Networking Arrangements Between Members and Financial Institutions

(a) Standards for Member Conduct

Except as otherwise provided in this Rule, a member that is a party to a networking arrangement under which the member conducts broker-dealer services on or off the premises of a financial institution is subject to the following requirements:

(1) Setting

A member that conducts broker-dealer services on the premises of a financial institution shall:

(A) be clearly identified as the person providing broker-dealer services and shall distinguish its broker-dealer services from the services of the financial institution;

(B) conduct its broker-dealer services in an area that displays clearly the member's name; and

(C) to the extent practicable, maintain its broker-dealer services in a location physically separate from the routine retail deposit-taking activities of the financial institution.

(2) Networking Agreements

(A) Networking arrangements between a member and a financial institution shall be governed by a written agreement that sets forth the responsibilities of the parties and the compensation arrangements and include all broker-dealer obligations, as applicable, set forth in Rule 701 of SEC Regulation R. Independent of their contractual obligations, members shall comply with all broker-dealer obligations, as applicable, under Rule 701 of SEC Regulation R.

(B) The member shall ensure that the written agreement stipulates that supervisory personnel of the member and representatives of the SEC and FINRA will be permitted access to the financial institution's premises where the member conducts broker-dealer services, as applicable, in order to inspect the books and records and other relevant information maintained by the member with respect to its broker-dealer services.

(3) Customer Disclosure

(A) At or prior to the time that a customer account is opened by a member that is a party to a networking arrangement, the member shall disclose in writing to each customer that the broker-dealer services are being provided by the member and not by the financial institution, and that the securities products purchased or sold in a transaction are:

(i) not insured by the Federal Deposit Insurance Corporation ("FDIC");

(ii) not deposits or other obligations of the financial institution and are not guaranteed by the financial institution; and

(iii) subject to investment risks, including possible loss of the principal invested.

(B) The disclosures required by paragraph (a)(3)(A) of this Rule also shall be made orally by a member that is a party to a networking arrangement for any customer account opened on the premises of a financial institution.

(4) Communications with the Public

(A) All member confirmations and account statements shall indicate clearly that the broker-dealer services are being provided by the member.

(B) Retail communications, including material published, or designed for use, in radio or television broadcasts, Automated Teller Machine ("ATM") screens, billboards, signs, posters and brochures, that announce the location of a financial institution where broker-dealer services are provided by the member or promote the name or services of the financial institution or that are distributed by the member on the premises of a financial institution or at such other location where the financial institution is present or represented shall include the disclosures required by paragraph (a)(3) of this Rule. The following legend may be used to provide these disclosures in retail communications, provided that such disclosures are displayed in a conspicuous manner:

- Not FDIC Insured
- No Bank Guarantee
- May Lose Value

(C) As long as the omission of the disclosures required by paragraph (a)(4)(B) of this Rule would not cause the retail communications to be misleading in light of the context in which the material is presented, such disclosures are not required with respect to messages contained in:

(i) radio broadcasts of 30 seconds or less;

(ii) electronic signs, including billboard-type signs that are electronic, time and temperature signs and ticker tape signs, but excluding messages contained in such media as television, online services or ATMs; and

(iii) signs, such as banners and posters, when used only as location indicators.

(5) Notifications of Terminations

A member shall promptly notify the financial institution if any associated person of the member who is employed by the financial institution is terminated for cause by the member.

(b) **Definitions**

For purposes of this Rule, the following terms shall have the meanings specified below:

(1) "Financial institution" shall mean federal and state-chartered banks, savings and loan associations, savings banks, credit unions, and the service corporations of such institutions required by law.

(2) "Networking arrangement" shall mean a contractual or other written agreement between a member and a financial institution under which the member offers broker-dealer services on or off the premises of the financial institution.

(3) "Broker-dealer services" shall mean investment banking or securities business as defined in Article I of the FINRA By-laws.

PART 721 - INCIDENTAL POWERS

§721.3 What categories of activities are preapproved as incidental powers necessary or requisite to carry on a credit union's business?

The categories of activities in this section are preapproved as incidental to carrying on your business under §721.2. The examples of incidental powers activities within each category are provided in this section as illustrations of activities permissible under the particular category, not as an exclusive or exhaustive list.

(c) *Finder activities.* Finder activities are activities in which you introduce or otherwise bring together outside vendors with *your* members so that the two parties may negotiate and consummate transactions and include vendors of non-financial products, vendors that are other financial institutions, and vendors of financial products such as insurance and securities. Finder activities may include endorsing a product or service, negotiating group discounts on behalf of your members, offering third party products and services to members through the sale of advertising space on your website, account statements and receipts, and selling statistical or consumer financial information to outside vendors to facilitate the sale of their products to your members. You may perform administrative functions on behalf of vendors to facilitate transactions between your members and another institution.

National Credit Union Administration

May 24, 2002

Guy A. Messick, Esquire
Lastowka & Messick P.C.
The Madison Building
108 Chesley Drive
Media, PA 19063-1712

Re: Registration of CUSOs Involved in Third-Party Brokerage Arrangements.

Dear Mr. Messick:

You have asked about the effect of the revision last year of our incidental powers activities rule on the need for credit union service organizations (CUSOs) to register as broker-dealers with the Securities and Exchange Commission (SEC) when they are involved in third-party brokerage arrangements for the sale of investments. 12 C.F.R. Part 721. As part of the revisions in that regulation, federal credit unions (FCUs) may now earn income from finder activities, such as third-party brokerage arrangements, which previously they could not do. 12 C.F.R. §721.6. Our understanding is that credit unions will continue to be exempt from registration but that the SEC is currently considering whether CUSOs will be exempt from registration because of the change in the incidental powers activities rule.

In 1993, the SEC issued a letter that authorized banks, thrifts, and credit unions to enter into third-party brokerage arrangements under certain conditions without the financial institution having to register. Letter from Catherine McGuire, Chief Counsel, SEC Division of Market Regulation, to Ian Celicia, Chubb Securities Corporation, November 24, 1993 (Chubb letter). The Chubb letter also said a "required service corporation" involved in such arrangements did not have to register.

NCUA Letter to Credit Unions No. 150 (Letter 150), issued in December 1993, provides guidance to credit unions about credit union related sales of nondeposit investment products and services, including third-party brokerage arrangements. It specifically recognizes that CUSOs may participate with a credit union and a broker in such arrangements. Letter 150 does not specifically address the necessity of registration with the SEC but states generally that credit unions must comply with all laws and regulations applicable to the activity.

We understand that various CUSOs engaged in third-party brokerage arrangements have considered themselves to be "required service corporations" and have relied on the Chubb letter to avoid SEC registration. The basis for the conclusion was that a CUSO was "required" in order for a credit union to earn income from the arrangement because of the previous limitation on compensation in Part 721. Our understanding is that SEC staff also held this view.

We have consulted with SEC staff about the elimination of the compensation limit in Part 721. SEC staff now questions whether CUSOs are still required service corporations, as that phrase is used in the Chubb letter, and whether CUSOs may continue to rely on the Chubb letter to avoid registration. As of the date of this letter, the SEC is still considering this issue. SEC staff has suggested that unregistered CUSOs should not form new, third-party brokerage arrangements pending an SEC decision on the matter. In addition, because the change in Part 721 only applies to FCUs, SEC staff is also considering whether there should be a distinction between FCUs and state-chartered credit unions because CUSOs of the latter may still be required in some states for a credit union to derive full monetary benefit from a third-party brokerage arrangement.

Credit unions may continue to engage in third-party brokerage activities and, except for the change on compensation for FCUs resulting from the change in Part 721, may continue to rely on Letter 150 as guidance. In addition, SEC staff informs us that, regardless of how the SEC determines the question of whether CUSOs must register, credit unions are and will continue to be exempt from registration if following the conditions of the Chubb letter. Credit unions and CUSOs involved in third-party brokerage arrangements where the CUSO is not registered should be considering what actions they will need to take if the SEC concludes the exemption in the Chubb letter no longer applies to CUSOs.

Sincerely
Sheila A. Albin
Associate General Counsel

02-0277

National Credit Union Administration

August 31, 2001

Fred M. Haden, General Counsel Navy Federal Credit Union
P.O. Box 3000
Merrifield, VA 22119-3000

Claude J. Kazanski, Assistant V. P. and Associate General Counsel
CUNA Mutual Group
P.O. Box 391
Madison, Wisconsin 53701-0391

Re: Sale of Nondeposit Investment Products by Dual Employees.

Dear Messrs. Haden and Kazanski:

In separate correspondence, each of you has asked if a federal credit union's (FCU's) employees may represent and perform work for a credit union service organization (CUSO) or other third party selling nondeposit investment products to the FCU's members. You also have asked if these investments may be sold on FCU premises too small to permit the physical separation of the investment sales from the FCU's deposit taking activities. The answer to both questions is a qualified yes.

You have indicated that CUNA Mutual Group (CUNA Mutual) has developed a program to sell nondeposit investment products to FCU members on the FCU's premises. The program contemplates having some FCU employees represent and work for CUNA Mutual or a CUSO as a shared employee on a part time, as-needed basis. You have stated that only properly trained and licensed employees will serve as shared employees.

You have also indicated that the program is structured to comply with the guidelines in the attached NCUA Letter to Credit Unions No. 150 (Letter 150) regarding the sale of nondeposit investment products. Letter 150 provides, among other things, that FCU employees may not offer investment advice. Accordingly, you have explained that the program is designed to make clear that when a shared employee is selling nondeposit investment products or providing investment advice, he will be doing so exclusively on behalf and under the control of the CUSO or CUNA Mutual and not in his capacity as an employee of the FCU. Neither the CUSO nor CUNA Mutual will pay the employee for his services; rather, they will compensate the FCU for the employee's time. Among other purposes, this will minimize the potential for conflicts of interest. We have no objection to this shared employee arrangement, provided the guidelines of Letter 150 are followed.

Letter 150 also provides that the sale of nondeposit investment products should be physically separated from the FCU's deposit taking activities to minimize member confusion as to the nature and risks of nondeposit investment products. Physical separation of these activities helps emphasize that significant differences exist between them, such as degree of risk and insurability. NCUA recognizes, however, that not all FCU offices are large enough to afford physically distinct office space in which to conduct these activities separately. We do not believe that this lack of space should preclude FCU members from enjoying the benefits of expanded member services if an FCU ensures that members receive appropriate disclosures.

Investment sales and deposit taking activities may be conducted in close proximity to each other where limited office space makes physical separation impractical, if appropriate disclosures are made when selling, advertising or marketing nondeposit investments. This includes disclosing in writing that nondeposit investment products: 1) are not federally-insured; 2) are not obligations of the FCU; 3) are not guaranteed by the FCU; 4) involve investment risk; and 5) if applicable, are being offered by an employee who accepts deposits on behalf of the FCU and also sells nondeposit investment products on behalf of the CUSO or other third party. These disclosures should be made in a location and type size that are clear and conspicuous to the member. These disclosures should also be made orally as part of any oral sales presentation.

You have indicated that the investment program

is designed to physically separate deposit taking and investment sales activities wherever practical. Where that is not practical, you have indicated that the program will meet Letter 150's disclosure guidelines enumerated above. In addition to the specific issues addressed above, you have indicated that the investment program will comply with all other guidelines in Letter 150.

Sincerely,

Sheila A. Albin
Associate General Counsel

01-0742

National Credit Union Administration

January 19, 2005

Mr. Philip Lieberman Linsco/Private Ledger
One Beacon Street, 22nd Floor Boston, MA 02108

Re: Providing Investment Services to Nonmembers

Dear Mr. Lieberman:

You have asked if a federal credit union (FCU) can provide investment services to nonmembers by using a shared employee with a broker-dealer. No, an FCU has no authority to provide investment services to nonmembers; using a dual employee does not change the limitation on FCU services to nonmembers. A shared employee, acting on behalf of the broker-dealer, could provide services to nonmembers but the FCU could not derive income from that activity. An FCU may invest in a credit union service organization (CUSO) that provides nonmembers investment services, or it may act as a finder of investment services to members under the incidental powers rule. 12 U.S.C. §1757, 12 C.F.R. §721.3(f). You have also asked if an FCU can provide broker-dealer services as a correspondent service to members of another credit union. No, an FCU may only provide correspondent services that fall under the express powers provisions of the Federal

Credit Union Act (the Act). The Act does not authorize FCUs to engage in broker-dealer services. 12 U.S.C. §1757.

Linsco/Private Ledger provides broker-dealer services to HFCU Services, Inc., a CUSO wholly-owned by Hughes Federal Credit Union (Hughes FCU). The CUSO currently provides investment services to both members and nonmembers of Hughes FCU. Under NCUA regulations, a CUSO may also serve nonmembers, as long as it primarily serves credit unions, their membership or the membership of credit unions contracting with the CUSO. 12 C.F.R. §712.3(b). By using a CUSO to offer investment services to members, Hughes FCU may derive income from HFCU Services, Inc. for the investment services to nonmembers. The CUSO is interested in expanding its business to serve members of other credit unions. Linsco/Private Ledger believes that it may contract directly with the FCU, rather than the CUSO, to provide broker-dealer services to members and nonmembers of Hughes FCU.

As we understand it, Linsco/Private Ledger would like to continue to provide broker/dealer services to its HFCU Services customers and expand the customer base to include members of other credit unions, but it would like to contract directly with Hughes FCU rather than HFCU Services. You ask whether Linsco/Private Ledger could do so by sharing an employee with Hughes FCU under a third-party networking agreement that would comply with NCUA Letter to Credit Unions No. 150 (Letter 150) and all other applicable rules. Hughes FCU may not circumvent the prohibition against serving nonmembers by using a dual employee. It could not profit from, or be reimbursed its expenses for, a dual employee's services to nonmembers. You argue that this arrangement would be consistent with our legal opinion OGC 01-0742, dated August 31, 2001. We disagree. In OGC 01-0742, we considered the permissibility of an FCU employee selling nondeposit investment products *to members* on behalf of a CUSO or third party. Id. Our opinion in that case does not permit a shared FCU employee to provide broker-dealer services to nonmembers. Further, Letter 150 does not authorize FCUs to provide broker-dealer services to nonmembers, it merely offers FCUs guidelines for otherwise permissible sales of nondeposit investment products.

You also suggest that an FCU could provide broker-dealer services to customers who are members of other credit unions as a correspondent service to the other credit unions. An FCU may only engage in activities that the Act expressly authorizes or that fall within an FCU's incidental powers. Correspondent services are a category of incidental powers in which an FCU provides services to other credit unions that it is authorized to provide to its members or as part of its operation. 12 C.F.R. §721.3(b). Under the incidental powers rule, an

FCU may earn income from incidental powers activities. 12 C.F.R. §721.6. As explained in the preamble to the most recent revision of the incidental powers rule, correspondent services are an exercise of an FCU's incidental powers because they are a convenient and useful way for a recipient credit union to carry out its *express* powers when it cannot perform the service itself. 66 Fed. Reg. 40845, 40850 (August 6, 2001). Since an FCU has no express power to provide broker- dealer services itself, it may only do so under another category of the incidental powers rule; as a finder activity. 12 C.F.R. §721.3(f). Finder activities permit an FCU to introduce members to third-party vendors so that the member and vendor may consummate a transaction. Id. An FCU may only engage in finder activities on behalf of members. An FCU cannot rely on the correspondent services category of incidental powers to provide a different category of services authorized by the incidental powers rule.

Sincerely,

/s/

Sheila A. Albin
Associate General Counsel

03-0736

NATIONAL CREDIT UNION ADMINISTRATION

Sales of Nondeposit Investments

AGENCY: National Credit Union Administration (NCUA).

ACTION: Proposed Interpretive Ruling and Policy Statement No. 05-1; with request for comments.

SUMMARY: The NCUA is proposing to adopt an Interpretive Ruling and Policy Statement (IRPS) on Sales of Nondeposit Investments. The proposed IRPS provides requirements, direction, and guidance to federally-insured credit unions on the establishment and operation of third party brokerage arrangements. The proposed IRPS updates and replaces NCUA's Letter to Credit Unions No. 150 on the sales of nondeposit investments.

DATES: Comments must be received on or before July 25, 2005.

ADDRESSES: You may submit comments by any of the following methods (Please send comments by one method only):

Sales of Nondeposit Investments to Nonmembers.
 Because credit unions may only provide services to members, a credit union may generally only accept income and pay expenses associated with nondeposit investment sales to its members. NCUA realizes, however, that in some cases it may be difficult for a credit union to connect particular income to a transaction involving a member. For example, some sales representatives may have generated sales that occurred before the representative joined the brokerage arrangement. These representatives may bring with them a stream of trailer income that cannot now be associated with any particular person or is not otherwise attributable to members of the credit union. A similar situation may arise in brokerage arrangements involving multiple credit unions working with one broker and sales made to members of the various credit unions.

 To address these situations, NCUA will allow a credit union in a third party brokerage arrangement to accept a *de minimus* amount of income that is not directly attributable to sales to its members. In this context, *de minimus* means that the ratio of income not directly attributable to members to the total gross income the credit union receives under the arrangement cannot exceed five percent.

A similar issue may arise if a credit union pays expenses associated with the sales of nondeposit investments. NCUA will allow a credit union in a third party brokerage arrangement to pay a *de minimus* amount of expenses associated with the sale of nondeposit investments to nonmembers. In this context, *de minimus* means that the ratio of nonmember sales expenses paid by the credit union to the total expenses paid by the credit union under the arrangement cannot exceed five percent.

[only the applicable section shown]

Protocol for Broker Recruiting

The principal goal of the following protocol is to further the clients' interest of privacy and freedom of choice in connection with the movement of their Registered Representatives ("RRs") between firms. If departing RRs and then new firm follow this protocol, neither the departing RR nor the firm that he or she joins would have any monetary or other liability to the firm that the RR left by reason of the RR taking the information identified below or the solicitation of the clients serviced by the RR at his or her prior firm, provided, however, that this protocol does not bar or otherwise affect the ability of the prior firm to bring an action against the new firm for "raiding." The signatories to this protocol agree to implement and adhere to it in good faith.

When RRs move from one firm to another and both firms are signatories to his protocol, they may take only the following account information: client name, address, phone number, email address, and account title of the clients that they serviced while at the firm ("the Client Information") and are prohibited from taking any other documents or information. Resignations will be in writing delivered to local branch management and shall include a copy of the Client Information that the RR is taking with him or her. The RR list delivered to the branch also shall include the account numbers for the clients serviced by the RR. The local branch management will send the information to the firm's back office. In the event that the firm does not agree with the RR's list of clients, the RR will nonetheless be deemed in compliance with this protocol so long as the RR exercised good faith in assembling the list and substantially complied with the requirement that only Client Information related to clients he or she serviced while at the firm be taken with him or her.

To ensure compliance with GLB and SEC Regulations SP, the new firm will limit the use of the Client Information to the solicitation by the RR of his or her former clients and will not permit the use of the Client Information by any other RR or for any other purpose. If a former client indicates to the new firm that he/she would like the prior firm to provide account number(s) and/or account information to the new firm, the former client will be asked to sign a standardized form authorizing the release of the account number(s) and/or account information to the new firm before any such account number(s) or account information are provided.

The prior firm will forward to the new firm the client's account number(s) and/or most recent account statement(s) or information concerning the account's current positions within one business day, if possible, but, in any event, within two business days, of its receipt of the signed authorizations. This information will be transmitted electronically or by fax, and the requests will be processed by the central back office rather than the branch where the RR was employed. A client who wants to transfer his/her account need only sign an ACAT form.

RRs that comply with this protocol would be free to solicit customers that they serviced while at their former firms, but only after they have joined their new firms. A firm would continue to be free to enforce whatever contractual, statutory or common law restrictions exist on the solicitation of customers to move their accounts by a departing RR before he or she has left the firm.

The RR's former firms is required to preserve the documents associated with each account as required by SEC regulations or firm record retention requirements.

It shall not be a violation of the protocol for an RR, prior to his or her resignation, to provide another firm with information related to the RR's business, other than account statements, so long as that information does not reveal client identity.

Accounts subject to a services agreement

for stock benefits management services between the firm and the company sponsoring the stock benefit plan that the account holder participates in (such as with stock option programs) would still be subject to (a) the provisions of that agreement as well as to (b) the provisions of any account servicing agreement between the RR and the firm Also, accounts subject to a participation agreement in connection with prospecting IRA rollover business would still be subject to the provisions of that agreement

If an RR is a member of a team or partnership, and where the entire team/partnership does not move together to another firm, the terms of the team/partnership agreement will govern for which clients the departing team members or partners may take Client Information and which clients the departing team members or partners can solicit. In no event, however, shall a team/partnership agreement be construed or enforced to preclude an RR from taking the Client Information for those clients whom he or she introduced to the team or partnership or from soliciting such clients.

In the absence of a team or partnership written agreement on this point, the following terms shall govern where the entire team is not moving (1) If the departing team member or partner has been a member of the team or partnership in a producing capacity for four years or more, the departing team member or partner may take the Client Information for all clients serviced by the team or partnership and may solicit those clients to move their accounts to the new firm without fear of litigation from the RR's former firm with respect to such information and solicitation, (2) If the departing team member or partner has been a member of the team or partnership in a producing capacity for less than four years, the departing team member or partner will be free from litigation from the RR's former firm with respect to client solicitations and the Client Information only for those clients that he or she introduced to the team or partnership.

If accounts serviced by the departing RR were transferred to the departing RR pursuant to a retirement program that pays a retiring RR trailing commissions on the accounts in return for certain assistance provided by the retiring RR prior to his or her retirement in transitioning the accounts to the departing RR, the departing RR's ability to take Client Information related to those accounts and the departing RR's right to solicit those accounts shall be governed by the terms of the contract between the retiring RR, the departing RR, and the firm with which both were affiliated.

A signatory to this protocol may withdraw from the protocol at any tune and shall endeavor to provide 10 days prior written notice of its withdrawal to all other signatories hereto A signatory who has withdrawn from the protocol shall cease to be bound by the protocol and the protocol shall be of no further force or effect with respect to the Signatory The protocol will remain in full force and effect with respect to those signatories who have not withdrawn.

National Credit Union Administration

November 14, 2001

Tom Whitmore, President/CEO
Lackland Federal Credit Union
2250 Kenly Avenue LAFB
San Antonio, Texas 78236

Re: Federal Credit Union as Licensed Insurance Agent.

Dear Mr. Whitmore:

You have asked if a federal credit union (FCU) may become a licensed insurance agent or if it is necessary for an FCU to invest in a credit union service organization that would offer insurance products to the FCU's members. An FCU may provide its members the opportunity to purchase a third-party vendor's insurance products as a permissible finder activity under our incidental powers rule. 12 C.F.R. §721.3(f). As such, an FCU may become a licensed insurance agent, if required under state law, in order to act as a finder of insurance products.

The NCUA Board has long authorized FCUs to offer vendors' insurance products to members. The 1985 amendments to our former insurance and group purchasing regulation permitted FCUs to accept compensation in excess of their administrative costs when offering insurance products incidental to providing an extension of credit. 50 Fed. Reg. 16462, 16463 (April 26, 1985). During that rulemaking, the preamble noted an FCU could be subject to state insurance laws, including individual agent licenses for FCU employees. Id. at 16464.

Recently, the NCUA Board replaced the insurance and group purchasing rules with a regulation that codifies permissible activities within an FCU's incidental powers under the Federal Credit Union Act. 12 C.F.R. Part 721. As part of the rulemaking, NCUA consolidated the former group purchasing and insurance activities under a category of incidental powers entitled finder activities. 65 Fed. Reg. 70526, 70530 (Nov. 24, 2000). Acting as a finder, an FCU introduces or otherwise brings together outside vendors with its members for the negotiation and consummation of transactions. 12 C.F.R. §721.3(f). The rule does not limit the types of vendors, products, or services an FCU may find for its members. Acting as a finder, an FCU may perform administrative functions for vendors and its members to facilitate their transactions, as previously authorized under group purchasing. Therefore, an FCU may act as a finder of insurance companies as a service to its members and earn income from engaging in finder activities, without restriction, under our rule. See 66 Fed. Reg. 40845, 40852 (Aug.

6, 2001) and 12 C.F.R. §721.6. An FCU, however, must comply with all applicable federal and local law. 12 C.F.R. §721.5. Therefore, an FCU could be subject to state insurance laws, including agency license requirements and restrictions on income.

Sincerely,

Sheila A. Albin
Associate General Counsel

01-0869

ABOUT THE AUTHOR

Guy A. Messick is an attorney with over thirty years of experience helping credit unions plan, organize and implement collaborations through credit union service organizations ("CUSO's"). He has counselled credit unions in every state and given presentations at over 100 meetings and conferences. His professional experience includes the following:

- General Counsel to the National Association of Credit Union Service Organizations and NACUSO's Regulatory Advocate 1987 – 2020.
- Founding partner in the law firm of Messick Lauer & Smith 1988 – 2020.
- Honored as one of the initial three CUSO Pioneers in America's Credit Union Museum in Manchester, NH.
- Guest presenter on collaboration at the University of Cork, Ireland and Pepperdine University, California.
- Author of *Credit Union Collaborations – Lessons Learned* and *The Guide for Credit Unions Providing Investment and Insurance Services*.
- Former Co-Chair of the American Bar Association's Credit Union Governance Sub-Committee.
- CUNA Investment Services Task Force Member

Guy lives in Media, Pennsylvania and Sarasota, Florida with his wife Lucy. They have five children and five grandchildren.

Although Guy will be retired from providing legal services effective January 1, 2021, Guy plans to continue to consult with credit unions and other cooperative organizations on how to create successful collaborations. He maintains a website called the CUSO Guru with articles and presentations, www.cuso.guru.

www.ingramcontent.com/pod-product-compliance
Lightning Source LLC
Chambersburg PA
CBHW030704220526
45463CB00005B/1897